small business handbook

an entrepreneur's guide to starting a business and growing a business

PHILIP WEBB & SANDRA WEBB

FINANCIAL TIMES
PITMAN PUBLISHING

FINANCIAL TIMES

MANAGEMENT

LONDON · SAN FRANCISCO
KUALA LUMPUR · JOHANNESBURG

Financial Times Management delivers the knowledge,
skills and understanding that enable students,
managers and organisations to achieve their ambitions,
whatever their needs, wherever they are.

London Office:
128 Long Acre, London WC2E 9AN
Tel: +44 (0)171 447 2000
Fax: +44 (0)171 240 5771
Website: www.ftmanagement.com

A Division of Financial Times Professional Limited

First published in Great Britain 1999

ISBN 0 273 63744 4

British Library Cataloguing in Publication Data
A CIP catalogue record for this book can be obtained from the British Library.

10 9 8 7 6 5 4 3 2 1

Typeset by Northern Phototypesetting Co. Ltd Bolton
Printed and bound in Great Britain by Bell & Bain Ltd, Glasgow

The Publishers' policy is to use paper manufactured from sustainable forests.

about the authors

Philip and Sandra Webb worked at IBM before spending the last ten years running their own businesses primarily in the computer services market place.

Their last business together was significantly successful because of its unique growth from start-up to £6.1 million turnover in just four years. This impressive growth for a small business was, amazingly, controlled organically without the need of investment during the recessionary years. The company was well recognized and acknowledged for its success and high standards in business methodology.

Philip Webb is now a Regional Councillor on the CBI East Midlands council and the Managing Director and owner of BDO Stoy Hayward Consulting Ltd, focusing on IT Strategy, European Monetary Union, Change Management and Year 2000 planning. Sandy and Philip Webb are currently writing the follow-up to the *Handbook*, entitled *Managing Change – How a Small Business Can Beat a Recession* and setting up the Entrepreneur's Club for small entrepreneurial businesses.

Philip and Sandra both manage and run their own smallholding in Derbyshire.

We would like to dedicate this book
to our dear daughters
SOPHIE AND MARIA

contents

foreword

Few would dispute that the will to survive has always been strong in the UK's small business community. But now, in an era when the only barriers to opportunity are the limits of our innovation and motivation, the will to survive must make way for the will to succeed.

According to recent Labour Force Survey figures, between 1979 and 1995, 1.8 m extra people became *self-employed*. Only 11 per cent, or 200,000 became *employers*. Of course, the specific reasons for such deficiency in business growth are manifold, but at the heart lies a fundamental weakness in the UK's enterprise culture.

This cultural deficit is perverse in its nature: opportunity is risk; business failure has a stigma far more powerful than the motivation to succeed. In the minds of many, young and not so, the risks of becoming an employer are yet too great when weighed against the comparative security employment can bring. This must change.

However, the greatest fear is fear of the unknown. Too many aspiring entrepreneurs lack skills necessary to steer a course around the obstacles that face every growing business, while at the same time grappling with the day-to-day headaches of producing, selling and getting paid.

While there is no substitute for real-life experience – getting out there and doing it – help is at hand in the form of information and advice from a range of sources. That is one of the key functions of the UK's 60 Approved Chambers of Commerce and it is the function of this book: practical guidance for business success.

Dr Ian Peters
Deputy Director-General
The British Chambers of Commerce (BCC)

introduction
the reality of entrepreneurism

Entrepreneurs are ordinary people with extraordinary determination.

What makes us want to become entrepreneurs? To get up in the morning and against all odds, carve a living out of nothing and grow a successful business?

> The feeling of self-worth that you develop as a business owner far outweighs everything else.

As an entrepreneur there can be tremendous responsibility on your shoulders to keep your company profitable and to maintain your banking and creditor relationships. You can feel totally alone, searching for the right answers with no mentor, no boss to appraise your work and no one to tell you to 'hang in there, you're doing a great job!'. Everyone around you expects you to have all the answers, but the problems still seem to manifest themselves into a myriad of conflicting needs.

But wait. There is nothing that compares to the feelings of freedom, creativity, and boundless energy brought about by running and growing your own business. Nothing can match that triumphant moment when you close a large or unexpected deal, the glow of satisfaction when you declare a profitable month, or the feeling of self-worth that you develop as a business owner.

■ Why have we written this book?

We know how hard it is in the first few years of running your own business. We have set up and managed three businesses in the last 10 years, giving us a vast pool of experience to draw on.

Our unique book with its accompanying diskette ▪ will provide you with essential information and advice, geared specifically to the entrepreneur. On the diskette you will find relevant and valuable documents in the form of real contracts, forms for a multitude of uses and action frameworks that you can adapt for your own business. If it helps you to use them do so, but please remember to get them checked by your own solicitor or accountant. What-ever happens, it will reduce your bill considerably or just give you examples for you to develop your own in-house forms/contracts.

Having sold our own company in 1996, we felt it necessary to write this book to demystify the theories of running a successful business. Like us, we are sure that you too, have searched high and low for a book offering practical guidelines and models for developing your business. This is *The* book that should have been available when we were starting out.

Running your own business is to assume high risk which then has to be controlled with a 100 per cent commitment and enthusiasm in order to ensure survival.

After working for a number of years in a large computer software organiza-tion, we felt that we were ready to move on and face the ultimate challenge of working for ourselves. It became a relatively easy decision for us to leave employment in 1990, though we were soon to learn that our drive and enthusiasm were no substitute for experience. With our combined skills, we felt we could offer a service to customers that they were currently not receiv-ing, setting up our own computer sales business with a heavy emphasis on free technical support and advice on installation.

> Times were good as we achieved numerous awards and business acknowledgements including ISO9002 and 'The Investor in People' award.

For the first 6 months, we worked until midnight, 7 days a week. We later converted our garage into a large office as the delivery of computers began to occupy the living space in the house. Eventually after our first year, which turned over £220 000, we moved to new premises and turned over £1.1 million in year 2 whilst increasing our staff to seven people. Our turnover increased to £3.2 million in the third year (turning our company into limited status) and £6.6 million in the fourth.

At this stage we employed 30 staff. During this rapid growth we searched for the correct way to structure departments and report lines. We will talk about how to cope with developing and managing company structures, adminis-tration and personnel later in Chapters 6 and 7.

Times were good as we achieved numerous awards and business acknowl-
edgements including IS09002 and 'The Investor in People' award. We had
fought through recession and made a business model work. It took more
than a year of costly mistakes and false starts before we finally got it right,
but during what we now consider to be the painful year preceding our success, we were able to learn the three fundamental lessons of business:

> **Lesson 1**: *Understand your customer and test your markets.*
>
> **Lesson 2**: *In retail, there are only three things that matter: location,
> location and location.*
>
> **Lesson 3**: *Never start a business in which you do not have a specialized
> knowledge, because it will probably fail.*

Later in the book we will show you how we achieved rapid growth and also
how to maintain it when cash flow is tight. In Chapter 2 we will show you
how you can plan your exit successfully from your business. Chapter 10
deals with disposals and acquisitions, which will give details about sale contracts, share swapping, mergers and acquisitions and how to watch you
don't get short-changed.

Each chapter will offer you the opportunity to design and create valuable
documents to help make your company run more smoothly and therefore
more successfully. Please help yourself become a better manager by working
through these documents and taking the time to study your own business in
more detail. In Chapter 4 you will find a detailed management training
course for you to test your new knowledge.

■ How to use this book

Each diagram, model and form in the book will either be in printed format
or be shown as a filename on your diskette. You will need Microsoft Office
97 in order to read these files. Full instructions for use are found in the file
on the diskette ■ **Readme.doc** file on the diskette . Each file is easy to access
and modify to a format for your own company's use.

Even if you have not yet started out in business, this book is the best friend
you will ever have! Read the early chapters to give you an understanding of
how to create the winning business plan, raise finance, and secure a flying
start for your venture.

If you have been in business for a while, please don't omit these sections. There is still a lot of work that you could probably do to alleviate future difficulties, just by following through on these steps. The creation of a stunning business plan, underpinned by a new shareholders' agreement, could be just the thing you need to help your business take steps to gain new heights.

Entrepreneurs, like ourselves, must have high energy levels to burn, which often means working long hours to ensure the business, once kick-started, keeps on moving, growing and developing. It's physically and mentally demanding and for those who are now thinking of starting a business, *take heed!*

The unrelenting pressures are there from day 1 until you exit, and if you think it will get better when you employ people, then think again. Every business owner that we have met, without exception, has cited the management of people as the most stressful part of managing their business.

Small companies are reluctant to benchmark with others due to time pressures and their need to retain their competitive edge. How can businesses ever hope to survive and grow successfully without learning from each other? If all businesses are going to learn by themselves and all go through the same hurdles time after time, it is no surprise that so many do not get through their first year let alone the second. It is a fact that 490 000 entrepreneurial companies set up each year, and only 90 000 of these will still be in business 5 years later. We firmly believe that, after reading this book, you will be one of those 90 000.

Small businesses must find the time to benchmark in order to find best practice. If you have an interest, please return the reply slip at the end of the book. We hope to set up an entrepreneurs' club to promote networking but, more importantly, benchmarking in your local area. If you haven't yet started in business, but would like to meet other entrepreneurs, feel free to return the reply slip anyway.

At this point, we would like to wish you and your company much success and hope that this book gives you strength and commitment to continue with your future challenges.

I may not have the answer, but I'll find it.
I may not have the time, but I'll make it.
I may not be the biggest, but I'll be the most committed.

preparing
the business

start out the way you plan to finish

Step 1: Shareholders' audit

Step 2: Shareholders' agreement and exit strategy

Step 3: Mission statement and goals

Coming together is a beginning, staying together is progress.
And working together is a success.

If only we had the foresight to have actioned this for ourselves when we started our computer services company in 1991. It is true to say that, if we had completed the activities in this chapter, we would have saved a tremendous amount of time and money.

It seems so obvious a series of steps to take, yet so few business owners, whom we have spoken to, have such a plan in place.

So what are we talking about? Three simple steps, which you must take for yourself, as early as possible in your business formation (see Fig. 1.1).

■ **Step 1: Conduct a shareholders' audit**
  In order to understand your personal requirements along with your own vision for the future.

■ **Step 2: Shareholders' agreement and exit strategy**
  If you are not the only shareholder, you must have in place a legal shareholders' agreement but, just as importantly, a statement of shared visions, goals, financial outcomes. This is derived from planning your exit.

■ **Step 3: Company Mission Statement and goals**
  The summation of Steps 1 and 2 will naturally lead to your being able to agree a vision for your company and allows you to set objectives to achieve your goals. This will provide the framework for your company's business plan which we talk about in Chapter 3.

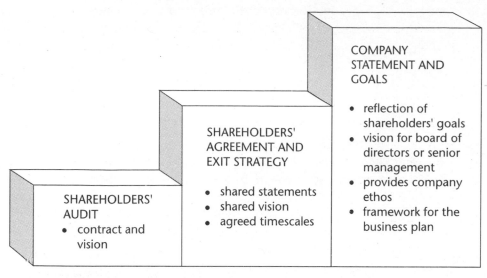

Fig. 1.1 THREE SIMPLE STEPS

preparing the business

STEP 1: SHAREHOLDERS' AUDIT

There are many books available that seek to try to analyze the personality traits of successful entrepreneurs and how to become one. One of the more unusual, yet enjoyable, books available is the *Victory Secrets of Attila the Hun* by Wess Roberts, PhD.

However, we are assuming you have already started in business and your real need is to understand your own position and its effect upon your ability to achieve greater success in your business. This extraction of personal information is relevant to the formation of a shareholders' agreement.

This may appear on the surface to be mere detail that bears little relevance since you are already trading. Let us assure you that it is every bit as relevant to you at this time. If the shareholders do not share congruent goals, or understand the goals of each other, conflict is waiting to happen. This is true even of husband and wife shareholdings, and this can become especially acrimonious due to the nature of the relationship.

If every business had a shareholders' agreement in place, then the potential for conflict and destructive behaviour would be greatly reduced. Don't forget, conflict at this level is both time-consuming and very costly to the business.

Inertia or lack of direction at a critical time in your business's development may stunt its growth irreversibly. This has a direct bottom line impact, and is the reason for our opening statement at the start of this chapter.

Work through the statements and record the information concisely on the prepared form available on the attached diskette [■ **Shareholders' Audit.doc**].

> *It is very important to note that you should never proclaim a statement of vision that you do not believe in, or one which is made just for effect. If the statements that you have made fail to become reality, the outcome can be worse than if you had not tried to communicate these statements at all.*

Then move on to the next section, where we will be looking at the structure of a shareholders' agreement, which will incorporate your completed form. We start this section by planning to sell the business that you have started, and the outcome will be a set of statements, objectives and goals that will be used in Chapter 2 : 'Plan your way to success'.

SHAREHOLDERS' AUDIT

Complete all sections as concisely as possible.

Your name.. Age.....................

The contract

1 Minimum gross salary required ....£............................. (per year/month)

2 Amount of your own money that you are prepared to stake in the business, either in cash or by way of guarantees secured on your assets.

    ....

3 What percentage equity do you hold?   ....per cent

4 How many other shareholders are there? ....

5 List their percentages ....

6 Do the other shareholders' retirement dates coincide with your own?

    ....

7 Does the shareholding split seem fair to you at this stage?............................

    ....

    ....

8 Indicate if there is a 50/50 shareholding split ....

    ....

9 Do you have a legal shareholders'contract in place?...................................

    ....

10 What would happen if the relationship between you and your other shareholders broke down irrevocably?

    ....

    ....

    ....

    ....

    ....

preparing the business

▶

11 How long do you want to work in your business and does it coincide with other shareholders' requirements? ....

....

....

....

....

12 Who should your shareholding go to in the event of your death? ....

....

....

13 In the event of the above, would you consider automatic sale of your shares back to the business for a pre-agreed sum, backed by insurance? ...

....

....

14 Describe the working and personal relationship between all shareholders.

....

....

....

....

....

15 What would you ideally like to earn on an annual basis? ....£ ....

16 Describe the additional benefits package. ....

....

....

....

17 What position would you like to hold in the company?...................................

....

Why? ....

....

18 Do you have an employment contract with your business (limited company only)?

....

....

19 What would your dividend policy be in order to distribute any profits, and what would the frequency be?..

....

....

....

The vision

20 Intended retirement date ....

21 Do you want to model the company for growth or profit?.............................

....

Why? ....

....

....

22 How big do you want your company to become?..

....

....

....

23 Describe your company in:

6 months ....

....

....

1 year ....

....

....

....

preparing the business

▶

9

3–5 years ....

....

....

....

10 years ....

....

....

....

24 What are your three main strengths and weaknesses in relation to achieving the above?

....

....

....

....

25 What is your Unique Selling Proposition that makes you different from everybody else in the market?

....

....

....

....

Do not use the words 'customer service' in this description.

26 Does your USP also address your customers' largest complaint about your marketplace?

....

....

27 Describe your company's set of values in relation to your customer.

....

....

....

....

....

28 Describe your company's report line structure and organization. Who reports to whom and does this work for you? ....

....

....

....

....

....

29 Describe the direction of the marketplace that you trade in. ....

....

....

....

....

30 Whom do you sell to? ....

....

....

....

31 Where is your largest opportunity for new business? ....

....

....

....

32 Any other relevant information? ....

....

....

....

....

preparing the business

STEP 2: SHAREHOLDERS' AGREEMENT AND EXIT STRATEGY

How peculiar! Planning to exit a business in order to take the business forward. How can this be? The point is this: if you understand exactly what you want out of your business, to the point where you can envisage your exit, the road to achieving this vision becomes a straight one.

> **Businesses can be run in many different ways.**

Businesses can be run in many different ways, often with no clear idea from the shareholders what it is they want to achieve. Most businesses will bumble along, year to year, paying salaries, trading with customers, paying suppliers, arguing with the bank. Then every new fiscal year, the cycle starts all over again. By deciding on the endgame, you are able to focus your business in the most appropriate way pertinent to your needs.

There are two main ways of styling your business.

The lifestyle business

Running the business until your retirement date – drawing a salary.

You are likely to pay yourself with a modest salary together with significant pension fund contributions, dependent on your profit levels each year.

A self-administered pension fund can deliver large taxation benefits, details of which are available from a competent tax accountant.

If your aims are long term, it is possible to retain earnings within the business, such that cash-flow is significantly eased, and the business over time will run more efficiently.

The 'grow to sell' business

Growing the business for an agreed fixed period to sell for a capital sum. This can be through a trade sale, a stock market flotation or a management buy-out/buy-in.

By far the more difficult and stressful of the two options. The commitment and energies required to achieving meaningful growth is exceptionally high.

The need to grow heightens and creates extraordinary pressures on cash-flow, skill shortages and people management problems. These risks often become acute and will need dedicated financial management, usually in the form of an in-house accountant or financial director. Please refer to Chapter 10: 'The point of disposal or acquisition', which will detail the different ways in which you can sell your business.

Payment of salary in a 'grow to sell' business is usually structured as a basic salary with incremental bonuses linked to achieved targets. See directors' service contract contained on the diskette [▪ Director's Contract.doc], which outlines a net profit bonus in a growth company. You will recall, that our computer services company was run in a 'grow to sell' style. In 1993 we had achieved impressive growth to £3.2 million and generated a healthy profit employing just 15 people. Looking back, our company at this time was relatively easy to run, simple to manage in people terms, and very flexible and entrepreneurial in its outlook.

Our bid for further growth increased our turnover to £6.6 million just 15 months later. The necessary financial controls, along with formalized management structures, increased our stress levels and reduced our enjoyment of the business. Twelve months later we sold the business for a capital sum that would have probably been matched by our dividends from the £3.2 million turnover business over a 5-year period.

> *In understanding the above, we would encourage you to consider carefully your motivators and your own personal limitations in relation to your exit strategy.*

The agreement

The shareholders' agreement can be compared to that of a personal will which is a combination of:

■ *a legal contract*
■ *your own personal vision and wishes.*

> The shareholders' agreement can be compared to a personal will.

Once all shareholders have completed their own audit forms, you can come together and reach an agreed position. An example of our shareholders' agreement can be found on diskette [▪ Shareholders Agreement.doc]. As you will have gathered by now, each shareholder's agreement is as bespoke as a personal will, but if our own example can provide you with working

preparing the business

13

clauses for your own ends, your solicitor's bill may be reduced.

The objective of having a legally binding shareholders' agreement is to protect the individuals, protect the business and document a common understanding of the requirements of the shareholders.

A document such as this is particularly valuable in the event that things go wrong. This may be the death of a shareholder, the parting of ways, either amicably or not, and ensures the business will continue.

The following points should be covered in the Shareholders' Agreement.

■ The contract

1 Reach written agreement on the legal questions raised in the self-audit.

2 Agree salary levels and the methods by which they will be changed in the future.

3 Agree a dividend policy.

4 Agree job titles.

5 Ensure service contracts are in place.

6 Restrict the sale of shares to any third party by any individual shareholder.

7 Discuss share swap insurance, which will pay a lump sum and force the estate of the deceased to accept this sum for exchange for the shares held.

8 If the shareholding is 50/50, make allowances for a deadlock clause. This is a method of blind bidding for the other shares in the event of irreconcilable dispute.

9 Ensure adequate arbitration clauses that give a clear-timed method of resolving disputes of all nature between shareholders.

10 The shareholders' right to appoint directors should be agreed.

11 The maximum number of shareholders can be agreed.

12 The frequency of board meetings should be stipulated, which should also state the quorum criteria.

13 The shareholders' right to access to financial information must be stated.

14 The memorandum and articles of association (in limited status companies) should be agreed.

15 All matters requiring consent of the shareholders should be stated, may include spending limits, borrowing limits, sale of assets, contractual matters and shareholders' interests in other business entities.

16 Any guarantees from shareholders must be documented.

17 Transfer of shares must be regulated through the provisions set out in the articles of association.

18 Distribution of profits should be agreed.

19 Assignment of shares must be restricted.

■ The vision

1 Reach written agreement on the vision and personal needs questions raised in shareholders' audit.

2 Agree on trading style, i.e. lifestyle or grow to sell business.

3 Define the exit dates, depending on agreement in No.11.

4 Produce a shared statement of values that the company will follow, and will be controlled by the board of directors (Ltd) or senior management team (partnership).

This can be summarized by your mission statement (see Step 3).

You should now take all of the above information to a competent solicitor and request that he formalizes your personal wishes and statements of shared visions, alongside the legal agreements you have made and produces for you a single shareholders' agreement.

Congratulations on completing this exercise. You have now accomplished more than most businesses and by doing so have increased your chances of success. Your business now has shareholders who agree on a wide range of issues, which leads to greater stability. You have also developed the ability to move to Step 3 which will take the outputs of all of the above, generate a company mission statement, and form specific objectives for your board of directors or senior management team to follow.

STEP 3: MISSION STATEMENT AND GOALS

There is an old saying: 'If you don't know where you are going, just about any path will get you there'.

Let's start this section by defining this word 'vision'. Vision or the mission statement is the company's intended activities, values and possibilities. It is a motivational statement as well as a descriptive statement and contains some of the emotion that will bind the business together as it moves forward.

This allows the company to empower its employees to support and work towards a common set of goals which is encapsulated in the mission statement.

The methods and processes contained in this chapter are the ones which have been developed for our own business and by which we successfully achieved the 'Investor in People' award in just 7 weeks!

The mission pyramid

The mission pyramid, shown in Fig. 1.2, summarizes this activity, but you will also notice that, if you work from the bottom of the pyramid, the summation of all of the individuals' objectives will eventually roll up to complete the mission statement.

Fig. 1.2 THE MISSION PYRAMID

■ Example of the mission pyramid at work

Mission statement

The company will address all computer-related requirements of our expanding customer base, to build long-term relationships and thus maximize return.

Company goals
- Expand in a controlled fashion.
- Maintain a cash-rich environment.
- Provide a quality service at all times.
- Continually develop existing and new marketplaces.
- Maintain ISO9002 Status.
- Develop product range in a researched fashion.
- Continually develop personnel through training.
- Maintain the 'Investors in People' award, which controls management theory and structure.
- Employ personnel in line with company expansion programme.
- Be leaders in our chosen markets.

Sales department

Goal
- To achieve the sales plan per year, as set by the board of directors.
- To maintain the ethos of service and quality at all times and to grow the name [Company] in the chosen marketplace.

Objectives
- Achieve gross profit sales targets.
- Build and maintain the professional image/reputation of the company.
- Operate an effective computerized sales reporting system.
- Manage and grow the sales in line with plan, developing new business opportunities.
- Manage the marketing activities to support sales plan and the engineering services of the company.
- Contribute to the positive cash-flow by setting contracts with favourable payment terms.
- Manage and recruit sales force to plan.
- Ensure all out-of-line situations are reported and handled correctly.
- Control assigned budgeting spend, making savings wherever possible.
- Adhere to *Manager's Handbook* with regard to company policies.

preparing the business

Sales manager objectives

Sales
- Achieve gross profit sales target as ratified by the board.
- Maintain and build the professional reputation of the company, ensuring your actions support the image of the company at all times.
- Manage and grow the sales department in line with the plan.
- Undertake marketing activities to support the sales plans.
- Contribute to positive cash-flow by setting contracts with favourable payment terms.
- Ensure the company's terms and conditions prevail at all times.
- Have an appointed sales manager or a replacement in training.

Administration
- Report to the MD in writing on a weekly basis to inform her or him of sales activity both current and intended.
- Ensure all out-of-line situations are reported to the MD.
- Control all assigned budgeting spend, making savings where possible.

Personal
- Expose yourself to entrepreneurial activities, working closely with the MD.
- Understand financial statements, organizational theory, the Companies Act 1985/89 and the company terms and conditions.
- Assume full responsibility for the company in the absence of the MD.
- Understand and assist with the business development function as a route to promotion.
- Manage and review your subordinates in a timely fashion, in line with the *Management Handbook*, ensuring personnel files are kept up to date.
- Complete TAM issues within 3 months.

To help you further, we have included a real job description relating to the finance function, which was successfully used in our computer services company. Feel free to copy it and develop for your own needs. [💾 **Job Example.doc**]

We conclude Step 3 by drawing upon the information already collated in our shareholders' audit, and summarizing this into a mission statement form to be found on the diskette under [💾 **Mission Statement. doc**] and company goals. This form is shown below, to help you achieve this final step.

The mission statement

The mission statement is taken from the shareholders' audit form from question numbers 22, 23, 25, 27, 30 and 31.

1 Summarize Question 23 using all the shareholders' completed forms.

2 Reflect upon the collective comments in Question 22.

3 Summarize in the following order Questions 30, 25, 27 and 31.

4 Rationalize the information that you have recorded in the steps above by condensing it into two to three sentences.

Congratulations, you have succeeded in producing your company's vision and mission statement! Move on to the next section where you will identify your company's specific goals, to be found on the diskette [**Goals Form.doc** which can then be cascaded down into your employees' job objectives.

The company goals

We suggest that, ideally, you produce between 7 and 10 company goals. Please refer to the mission pyramid. This will focus the business upon the *strategy* rather than on the *operations*, which are dealt with in the departments and individuals' objectives. Remember, the summation and, indeed, the individual goals must all relate to the mission statement generated.

You should consider a mix of goals relating to your company's departmental functions, but specifically with regard to finance, sales, marketing, customer, quality and technical/legal.

Once again, we are going to refer to that very valuable document, the shareholders' audit, and this time consider the answers to the following Questions: 2, 11, 19, 21, 29 and 31. Use the spaces provided below to draft your company goals in a concise manner.

preparing the business

1 Using Question 2, you can determine your financial position and if required generate a specific goal relevant to financial control.

2 Question 11 relates to timescales by which the business must achieve your vision. Ensure goal achievements match timescales.

3 Question 19 relates to financial goals, with an emphasis on division of profits.

4 Question 21 will generate a goal, which stimulates growth.

5 Question 29 and 31 relate to business development, which you may wish to focus upon.

From this mission statement and company goals, we can then show you how to draw down the department goals and to communicate these goals in the form of specific objectives to the entire company. This process is detailed in Chapter 7: 'Managing people'.

Well done, you have completed Chapter 1. This information gathered will be used to write your business plan, along with your sales forecasting and cash-flow projections.

By changing your goals, you can adjust your direction.

PRACTICAL STEPS

■ Reduce the potential for conflict by developing your shareholders' agreement.

■ Publish your shareholders' agreement and copy to all shareholders to achieve a common understanding and direction.

■ Using your vision statement, you have extracted the company's goals and objectives to provide a framework for your business plan.

■ You have now built a stable foundation from which to grow your business.

plan your way
to success

The business plan matrix

This chapter is all about business planning. It may not appear to be the most exciting subject in the world, but the working sheets we have provided for you will change all of that.

> **In business it is vital that your plan is good, and current.**

In the absence of a good plan, the battle is often lost, and in business it is vital that your plan is good, and current. Business plans are live and inspirational documents that you can use for a whole variety of purposes. We used ours on a quarterly basis, and the models of profit were updated every month. Once you have worked through this chapter, you will be enlightened as to how useful and exciting the planning part of your business has become.

You will discover how to:

- compile a professional business plan using a standard provided template
- produce a full profit and loss model of your business using the Excel workbook provided
- produce an automated cash-flow worksheet provided
- embrace the planning process as a fundamental part of your business.

Two stone cutters were asked what they were doing. The first said, 'I am cutting this stone into blocks.' The second replied, 'I'm on a team that's building a cathedral.'

Which stone cutter would you invest your money in? They both do precisely the same job, but one is perceived to have a vision and a more successful future than the other. The same is true to say, when you approach your bank manager. His first question will be, what do you do? What will your answer be?

We hope that you won't have to think too hard about this question, since in the previous chapter you have made your mission statement and company goals from your shareholders' agreement. However, the bank manager will ask for more than this when appraising his lending risk to your business. Of course, what we are talking about here is a business plan.

To produce a good business plan is not simply to regurgitate information just to satisfy the basic requirements. If you put enough thought into the production of your plan, it can make quite an amazing difference in the way your business will run.

As a prime example, we would like to tell you how our own business plans had a tremendously positive effect on the growth of our business. In our start-up phase, we had £250 of our own money. By producing a coherent business plan, which was well thought-out, structured and with budgets and cash-flow forecasts attached, we were able to raise a £5000 *unsecured* overdraft facility.

Our business grew at a phenomenal rate and operating capital via overdraft facility was always top of our agenda. Many companies at this stage would have felt starved of cash, or the directors would have been forced to produce *personal guarantees* in support of their business's borrowing. Our business, in fact, grew from start-up to over £6 million in 4 years. At the end of the fourth year, we were using a £300 000 overdraft, for which the only security was our sales debtors. *Our business planning was the prime reason why we have never had to offer personal guarantees or to jeopardize our personal assets in support of our business.*

Rule 1: *Planning is vital for your company's health and financial success.*

Before we go on to look at how you too can develop a professional business plan, let us examine the reasons why the plan is being written in the first instance.

Which of the following do you think are valid reasons:

■ to satisfy your bank manager?

■ to satisfy other investors?

■ to show to prospective customers?

■ to discuss with your suppliers?

■ to use in your board meetings?

■ to discuss with your management team?

■ to introduce additional investors?

If you said 'yes 'to all of the above, you are correct.

preparing the business

But hang on, I hear you say, I would never discuss the same business plan with my bank manager as I would with my customer or supplier. And, again, you are absolutely correct. It is common sense that you will show your customer or supplier a cut-down version of the original plan so that your customer/supplier can have faith in your business's ability and future direction.

The next part of this chapter will focus on the structure of the business plan and suggested information that you should provide within each section. It is shown as a heading followed by a series of questions that you may wish to consider, when completing each section.

A full example of our own working business plan can be found on the diskette [■ **Business Plan.doc**]. This document can be used in whole, or part, in support of your own business plan, or alternatively you may like to use the format given below.

The net result of the business plan is to give you a working set of projections for the sales and expenditure of the business. As anyone knows who has tried to formulate such a model, it can be a very complicated exercise as your company grows larger.

We have therefore provided for you a complete *working Excel Workbook*, whose titles you can change to suit your business. This allows you to input, and model to fine detail, monthly variations in sales, profit, expenditure, salaries, etc. This will turn the process of planning into an enjoyable experience of modelling, and will hopefully become an invaluable aid to you on a monthly basis. You can find this model on the diskette [■ **Planning.xls**].

Finally, the sexy bit! This is the piece of the jigsaw all banks want and hardly ever get, all boards of directors want but rarely see. It is, of course, the cash-flow statement. Our cash-flow file has automatic links, which, if you reconnect on your own system, will be automatically updated from the planning *Excel Workbook*. To our knowledge, this is not commercially available unless you invest in some very expensive modular accounting software. Again, this model is on the diskette [■ **Cash Flow.xls**].

After the business plan matrix, we have illustrated some example sheets from the above spreadsheets (*see* pp. 33–5).

> **Rule 2:** *Planning is like a map. If you take the time to plan your route before you set off, you can save a lot of time along the way.*

THE BUSINESS PLAN MATRIX

The following is an alternative approach to the development of the business plan, based upon a *'prompting' system that you can use to ease the writing of your outline business plan.*

■ Avoiding overkill

This sample matrix covers a lot of ground. You don't have to answer every question to have a top-notch business plan. You do, however, need to address most of them. Sometimes the need to address a point will depend upon whether you produce a product or a service. In either case, read the point and carefully consider if you have, or need to have, addressed the issue in your own mind and in the pages of your business plan.

■ Repetition

There are a number of instances where you are required to repeat yourself between the executive summary and other chapters. While frustrating, this tradition with business plans is necessary, since a number of readers (your bank manager, an investor, etc.) will skip the rest and turn only to the part that interests them. If you keep each chapter too skimpy, you could fail to impress an important reader.

■ Differing advice

Friends and colleagues will refer you to a number of different approaches in compiling your business plan. It can be said that while there are many wrong ways to do a business plan – there is no exclusively right way. The following represents an approach that has proved to be tried and true for many new entrepreneurs. Your ability to use it as a guide, and modify it to your own use, is what will make it work for you.

The title page

This should be attractive and 'visually literate' so that it invites the reader to proceed. It should contain the name of the product or the service and the name of the company. It should always be marked *confidential*. It may pay you to get a local service to design and print your cover page as well as bind the publication in coil binding to facilitate easy reading.

preparing the business

The executive summary

The executive summary is always done last *after* the overall plan has been completed and polished to cover all details. The summary should not exceed 4 or 5 pages.

Content of executive summary

- A paragraphed statement designed to create *instant interest* in the idea, the potential and the vision of the owner/creator
- Purpose of the business
- Current stage of the business
- Legal status of business (partnership, limited company, etc.)
- Key management personnel
- A brief overview the industry
- The customer, customer needs, product benefits and target markets
- Major competitors and strengths
- Venture capital required including development, operations and marketing
- How much investment? When will it be paid back?
- How long to break even?
- What capital invested to date?
- The important and distinct functions of the business.

The concept

What's so special about your product or service?
This section should cover everything that makes your product or service unique as compared to current competitors or their ways of doing things. If it is a manufactured item, emphasize the uniqueness by describing all patents, formulas, brand names or other copyright strategies.

What innovative technology do you use?
Sometimes it's not the product that's unique, but the process of manufacturing. For example, the now famous 3M yellow sticky notes. Sticky pads have always been around, the trick with the 3M product is the fact that the glue doesn't dry, enabling them to be used over and over again.

Category of business?
Are you a manufacturer, retailer, distributor or service provider? Explain which of these or other services you offer and the details of your service.

The intended customer?
Who comprises your target market? Specify the need that you will fill and be sure to include their profile.

What are the customer benefits? What problems are you solving for them?
The wisest thing ever said about customer need is 'your customer must not only need the product – he must know that he needs it'.

Who will create the product?
Will it be manufactured overseas or locally? How will you protect yourself against unforeseen problems in assuring supply? The difference between a product and service is not as great as some would imagine.

> **Will you be the salesperson as well as the producer?**

How will the product be sold?
Will it be offered locally, nationally, or internationally? Will you be the salesperson as well as the producer? If so, who will run the business while you are out there selling?

The product plan

- Describe the purpose of the product.
- Detail the 'unique selling proposition' (USP). A Unique Selling Proposition is what makes your product different from every other.
- What is the current stage of development?
- Prototype, market ready, or just a concept?
- How was the product developed?
- By you? Is it a franchised item or service? Are you a reseller?
- What is the shelf-life or the so-called 'window of opportunity'?
- How will the product be produced?
- Is it capital intensive, labour intensive, material intensive?
- Will any part of it be subcontracted?
- If so, to whom – and with what safeguards?
- What future research and development is needed?

preparing the business

■ Even though it may be ready for the market today, will changes be needed to reflect changing technology in the near future?

■ What licence or royalty agreements are in place?

■ If you don't own the product, the publication, the software, etc. whom do you have to pay for its use and how will you protect yourself?

■ What government approvals are needed?

■ What are the potential liabilities?

■ And how will you indemnify yourself? What about insurance – and its cost?

Resource plan

■ To introduce this section, an overview of the type of goods or services offered should be reiterated.

■ Breakdown of inventory/people: details such as what, where and the volume, plus the cost of maintaining necessary levels of stock.

■ Where will inventory/people be obtained?

■ What are terms of purchase, employment, lease returns, etc.?

■ What lead times are necessary for you to get the product from inventory to reseller to customer?

■ Where will the customer make the purchase, e.g, direct mail, retail stores, catalogues, etc.?

Management team

■ This section calls for a demonstration of the competency of the senior team.

■ It is vital that this is shown clearly and must include *overview* CVs of all directors with all relevant experience shown. Full CVs should be appended.

■ A table of shareholdings and options against director/manager will allow the investor to see the commitment.

■ A structural chart can be shown and can also indicate vacancies and future expansion, clearly showing the planned management lines of control.

■ Job descriptions and objectives of the positions will enable rapid understanding of the strength of management and the focus on output-led results.

■ Be candid as to any areas where you have a weakness or a skill gap. The investor or bank will understand a hiring need, but not appreciate a fudging of incompetency.

Competition

- List direct competitors by product and geographic market.
- Describe competitor strengths and weaknesses.
- Describe competitors' share of the market.

Who are your indirect competitors?

- Discuss any relevant background information concerning competitors.
- On what basis will you compete with competitors?
- How is this venture or idea superior to that of the competitor?
- Does this threaten the major strategic objectives or the image of the competitor?
- If the competitors threaten to destroy your market position, how will you respond?
- Who are your indirect competitors?

Pricing

- Design a pricing sheet for customers, listing various options (if you have more than one). Compare your pricing to that of your competitors.
- What are your pricing policies in meeting the competitors? In other words, what is your fall-back position if they try to force you out of the market by cutting their profit margins?
- Understand and recognize the effect of currency fluctuations in your selling and purchasing activities.
- If you are importing the product, describe the process and brokerage, duties, etc.
- Describe your prices as they relate to your costs, and the price that the market is able to pay.

Marketing

Prioritize the market.

- Describe the industry's current market. How will you fit into it?
- Describe the benefits of the product/service.
- What are the customer's needs that you fill? Does he know he needs the product?

preparing the business

- Describe the collective target market and the potential volume in terms of sterling/dollars.
- Prioritize the market. Where are the best financial returns and the next, etc.?
- List the costs for each market segment.
- What advertising/marketing strategy will be used? Demonstrate that this is the most effective one possible, in terms of targeting your customer.
- What are the costs of such advertising? Who will produce your ads, and at what cost for artwork, writing, etc.?
- What service support, warranties, and guarantees must you offer?
- What market research has been done – and with what results?
- What experience do you have in marketing? Or, if not, whom will you turn to?
- How will your marketing differ from that of competitors?
- What role will trade shows play?
- How can you use other companies to promote your product/service? Perhaps you can work out reciprocal arrangements.
- What are the future markets as the available technology changes?
- How will you stay in touch with developments in your industry, e.g. joining trade clubs, conferences, etc.?

Operating and control systems

- What is the process for receiving and processing orders?
- Explain administrative policies, procedures and controls.
- Make a graphic of the process. (Schematics make it easier for readers to understand what's in your mind.)
- What documentation is needed for a transaction?
- What role will IT play in delivering controls?

Contingency plans

What if ...
- sales projections prove wrong?
- supply deficiencies occur?
- government interference arises?
- product liability problems arise?

- problems with management, personnel or partners arise?
- Are there statements of risk such as exposure to Year 2000 millennium issues and European Monetary Union?

The financial deal

This is the section where we have in the past thrown all of the details over our shoulders to our accountant, with instructions to complete! However, to give specific instructions, it is necessary to understand what it is you need. This section, along with the files, will provide an understanding of the work required. See Chapter 9 for advice as to how to appoint and then manage your accountant. If you have the time, and want to learn about the financial deal, then read on. We have simplified the language and the forms and files as well.

> It is necessary to understand what it is you need.

- What (how much and what type of) capital is required for the start-up and beyond for the first 3 years?
- If the funds come from debt, what collateral is being offered as security?
- What funds will be injected by outside investors and what will they demand/receive in return?
- What leases, loans and other liabilities will/do exist?
- What tax benefits will be provided to you and investors?
- What government loans, guarantees or grants can you call upon?

Financial information

Perhaps the most important part of the business plan, and often the most neglected, is the section dealing with financial controls and projections. This section deals with the specific details and requires the analysis that can only be shown using spreadsheets.

■ The opening balance sheet

An opening balance sheet has two sides: one side showing the money that you have, or intend to invest in leasehold improvements, equipment and machinery, vehicles and recurring start-up expenses. The other side details the financing you will need: for instance, term loans, owner's equity, founders' investment or outside investors.

■ The operating statement

This shows projected sales and expenses. It estimates the profitability of the business over a specific period of time. This may be the first 12 months of the new business or longer, and, to be credible, should reflect a slow start followed by reasonable growth.

■ The cash-flow statement

Nothing kills a business faster than poor cash-flow. A cash-flow statement shows all the cash that you expect to receive, placed in the month that you expect to receive it. It also shows all the bills you anticipate in the specific month in which you expect to pay them. A cash-flow is not an estimate of your sales and expenses, but an estimate of when the money associated with the sales will be received and when the money involved with paying for expenses will be paid.

> Nothing kills a business faster than poor cash-flow.

Appendices

To include:

- Full CVs of all relevant directors and senior personnel
- Historic accounts of the company
- Reconstruction of the balance sheet, naming the extraordinary costs involved and the reason for their discounting
- Marketing information including customer testimonials to show the successful company so far
- Brochures relevant to the opportunity.

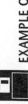

EXAMPLE OF A WORKING CASH-FLOW FORECAST

	Jan	Feb	March	April	May	June	July	Aug	Sept	Oct	Nov	Dec	Total
Projected sales													
Cash receipts (cash in)													
Sales invoiced													
Collections from accounts receivable													
Owner's capital													
Loan proceeds													
Other cash received													
Total cash In	0	0	0	0	0	0	0	0	0	0	0	0	0
Cash disbursements (cash out)													
Purchases (cost of consultants and direct expenses)													
Advertising													
Cars (incl. insurance)													
Bank charges													
Invoice disc charges													
Loan interest													
Insurance (business liability)													
Professional fees (accounting and legal)													
Rent (equipment)													
Rent (premises) + rates													
Miscellaneous costs													
Telephone and fax													

preparing the business

EXAMPLE OF A WORKING CASH-FLOW FORECAST (continued)

Utilities											
Repairs and maintenance											
Marketing											
Travel and promotion											
Wages (employees and payroll deductions)											
Management salaries											
Loan payments (capital not interest)											
Purchase fixed assets											
Taxes (Income)											
Office supplies and expenses											
Subsistence											
Audit											
Miscellaneous											
Bad debts											
Total cash out	0	0	0	0	0	0	0	0	0	0	0
Cash-flow summary											
Opening balance	0	0	0	0	0	0	0	0	0	0	0
Add: Cash in	0	0	0	0	0	0	0	0	0	0	0
Subtract: Cash out	0	0	0	0	0	0	0	0	0	0	0
Surplus or (deficit)	0	0	0	0	0	0	0	0	0	0	0
Closing cash balance	0	0	0	0	0	0	0	0	0	0	0

COMPANY NAME

OPENING BALANCE SHEET

Date: September 1997

ASSETS

FIXED ASSETS

Land and buildings	£0.00
Furniture, fixtures and equipment	£41 544.00
Automobiles	£0.00
Leasehold improvements	£0.00
Other assets/intangibles	£0.00
TOTAL FIXED ASSETS	£41 544.00

CURRENT ASSETS

Cash and bank accounts	£96 731.00
Debtors	£170 055.00
Stock/inventory	£0.00
Pre-payments	£0.00
Other current assets	£0.00
TOTAL CURRENT ASSETS	£266 786.00
TOTAL ASSETS	£308 330.00

LIABILITIES

CURRENT LIABILITIES

Creditors	£209 875.00
Bank loans	£0.00
Loans – other	£0.00
Current portion of long-term debt	£0.00
Other current liabilities	£0.00
TOTAL CURRENT LIABILITIES	£209 875.00
ASSETS LESS LIABILITIES	£98 455.00

LONG-TERM LIABILITIES

Mortgages and liens payable	£0.00
Other loans of long-term nature	£39 651.00
Less: current portion	£0.00
TOTAL LONG-TERM LIABILITIES	£39 651.00
TOTAL LIABILITIES	£249 526.00
NET ASSETS	*£58 804.00*

OWNERS' EQUITY	£50 000.00
Profit and loss account	£8 804.00
Capital investment	
TOTAL	***£58 804.00***

PRACTICAL STEPS

In this chapter we have shown you how to:

■ Write a successful business plan which will enable you to communicate the purpose and direction of your business to the various institutions such as banks, investors, customers and creditors.

■ Produce a profit and loss model of your business which gives you the ability to model 'what if' scenarios and plan variances.

■ Derive the benefit of an automated cash-flow workbook which allows you to predict the cash requirements of the business based on the variables in the profit and loss model.

Remember, planning is a worthwhile task. Set aside time for it. Model your figures using the spreadsheet, copy them and then play with various scenarios. Write your business plan and update it every year, but make it the best plan you have ever written.

The plan and the models, after all, are your business, so be proud of them, use them, and have fun planning and measuring your business for maximum control.

If you have found some difficulties in understanding the terminology and rationale behind the business modelling and cash-flow spreadsheets, worry not. In Chapter 4 we will be examining this in greater detail by taking you through the four most important training modules *en route* to a successful business.

so you want to own an office?

Types of premises available
Lease, rent or buy?

The true measure of success is not what you have, but what you can do without.

It is the most natural reaction in the world to put as the first item on your list the desire to open business premises. So many times we see that the small business owner places far too much focus on this activity as a way of demonstrating to all around him (including himself), that he has a tangible and viable business.

> **This chapter is dedicated to saving you time and money!**

All too often, in the rush to secure a building, many important factors are overlooked which can cost the business owner dear. In some cases that we have witnessed, the commitment to maintaining payments (either mortgage or lease) can have a crippling effect on the financial stability of the company.

This chapter is dedicated to saving you time and probably a significant amount of money! We will guide you through the maze of choices relating to such things as:

- defining the need for your premises
- types of premises available
- how technology can save you money
- to lease, rent or buy?
- grant assistance
- negotiating terms
- break clauses.

Whatever choices you make, you must be clear that this will have a very marked effect upon your company.

If at this stage you are about to purchase, or thinking about purchasing a business with *incumbent* business premises, please read this chapter first and then move on to Chapter 10: 'The point of disposal or acquisition', which spells out the pitfalls associated with either buying a business or selling and therefore disentangling from your own.

Many businesses, with the exception of the retail sector, often start out being located in a bedroom, garage or workshop. This has the advantage of carrying nearly zero overheads, as the individual usually owns these premises to start with. Our own computer services company started trading from a single spare bedroom, with two telephone lines and a second-hand desk. We then converted our double garage to a five-desk office which served us extremely well in the first 2 years of our company. The only reason why we moved into commercial premises was to satisfy *our need* to physically expand the business.

It is worth noting at this point that the turnover of our business at the point at which we moved into new premises was just over half a million pounds. So, you see, turnover should not be a deciding factor in your decision. Your decision to own premises must be a clear one, based upon fact and not merely on contemplation. We will now look at the factors that you must consider when making this vital decision.

The need for premises

We've constructed a checklist that you may wish to use when deciding either whether to move premises or indeed to confirm your existing premises are satisfactory. If you are selling through a shop front to the general public and rely on passing trade, move to the third bullet point.

THE NEED FOR PREMISES CHECKLIST

■ In understanding who your customer is now, and who they will be in the future, what exactly does your *customer* require of your business premises?

 – Will your customer want to visit you often?

 – Do you require demonstration facilities?

■ If you are in manufacturing, distributing or processing, work out the size of the non-office environment space that you require and that you project to require in the future. Refer to your business plan in Chapter 2.

■ Do you feel that your proposed location (or existing location) is prohibiting you from hiring or retaining the best staff in the labour market?

 – Is this due to location or proximity to town centre?

 – Is this due to the style or standard of your building?

■ In considering your business's expansion, can you foresee the time when your business may need to relocate again?

 – Can you project a timescale for the above?

■ Can your business afford to make a significant capital down payment on a business, or would it be better to see a minimal down payment but slightly larger quarterly outgoings?

Take your time to answer the above questions and don't let your ego take over the decision-making process.

The answer to paragraph 1 we believe is the most important; after all, it is the customer who generates your revenue and pays your wages. It is very natural for the customer's needs to pre-empt your own wishes or that of your partners.

If your answers from the checklist have firmed up your intentions to locate to new premises, read on to identify the options you have when making your selection of buildings.

TYPES OF PREMISES AVAILABLE

Retail

If you own a business in the retail sector, your choice of premises becomes fairly obvious. We would, however, like to point out that many specialized retail businesses transact the majority of their business by means other than customers visiting their shop. For more advice on how you can explore this possibility further, see Chapter 5: 'Sales and marketing strategies'.

If you are customer-facing and require passing trade to generate your income, we will simply underline the well-known message, Location, Location, Location!

In our own retail experience, which we discussed in the Introduction, we undertook a passing trade survey, which counted the number of people passing the proposed retail unit. We found that 200 people per minute passed the proposed retail unit door, which was based in a new arcade outside the main city centre.

Once we had opened our retail outlet, we found that 200 people a minute still passed our door, but unfortunately very few of them actually entered the new arcade. Analyzing this position sometime afterwards, a management consultant pointed out two simple facts.

Fact 1: The arcade did not allow pedestrians a walk through to get to other main shopping attractions, and it became just as easy for the shoppers to walk around the building instead of through it.

Fact 2: It was located 500 yards outside of the main city shopping area (a 5-minute walk).

People will not go out of their way to visit even your shop. Indeed, we have found by talking to other shop owners that one side of the High Street may be extremely busy, due to a bank or bakeries, whilst the opposite side of the street struggles to make a living, simply because people cannot be bothered to cross the road.

> People will not go out of their way to visit your shop.

Industrial

If you already own or proposing a business in manufacturing that uses heavy plant machinery, then your choice of premises becomes restricted to type A1 use. This term is derived from the local councils' planning process by which certain types of buildings are only suitable for heavy manufacturing types of operation.

We would suggest that you take advice from commercial estate agents as to the type of A1 properties available and whether other non-industrial buildings (type A2) may be the subject of a planning application to turn them into A1 premises.

If you are involved in manufacturing, it is likely that factors such as ease of access to main trunk roads, railways and airports may be a key consideration. If you are relocating your business, there may be substantial financial assistance available to support your purchase of capital equipment and safety equipment. This can be found by contacting your local Business Link or economic development department of the city or county council.

Commercial premises

As stated above, these are usually classified as A2, which means that they can be used for light manufacturing, assembly, distribution and offices. This is by far the most common type of property available, with the greatest range of style and design. Clearly, a distribution business will also require an infrastructure of communications, including access to motorways, airports and railways.

preparing the business

Our own computer services company was based in an A2 building which was initially very inexpensive to lease because only 10 per cent of the area was built into offices. The remainder was a concrete storage floor extending full height into a steel girder roof. We knew that our expansion would call for a greater office area, but offices generally in the city would cost about £9 per square foot.

Over the following 2 years, we had a wooden mezzanine floor installed and a total of five large offices built using stud walling and false ceilings. This area eventually accommodated 20 employees in 4500 square foot for a cost of £4 per square foot. A one-off capital cost for this refurbishment was a total of £9500, a saving of £13 000 in the first year and £22 500 savings every year thereafter, as a result of the above decision.

> *Tip 1*: *Use your imagination when considering suitable premises, as this can save you a tremendous amount of money in the long term.*
> *Tip 2*: *You must try to build flexibility into your selection, as you will encounter change of needs as your business grows.*

During our expansive years in this simple building, we had no need for the customer to visit us and therefore our physical image was less important. As our business continued to enlarge, our customers began to require demonstrations of our equipment and services, which meant regular meetings at our offices.

It was this factor alone that prompted us to select a building with prestige value as opposed to a larger, similarly styled unit to our existing offices. However, in finding the right premises we encountered difficulties. We had a need for good, clean offices, with an engineering area, storage and distribution areas. This mixed-use building is the most expensive on the markets, and so we thought and planned in advance and used our creative imagination.

We eventually selected a prestigious office block on three floors and negotiated with the landlord to allow us to incorporate our non-office functions within the office block. The net result was a good financial deal: all the functions of the company in the same building, and a very impressive, fully carpeted warehouse operation.

> *Tip. 3*: *Don't accept the stated; negotiate the deal that **you want** and if you don't get it, be prepared to move on.*

Design build

To many people, the prospect of designing and building your own premises from scratch is immediately rejected on the basis of perceived high cost. This is not necessarily the case. It is certainly possible to explore this option on a free-of-charge basis with the developer. Units as small as 2500 square foot can be purchased on a design and build basis. Indeed, most developers will explore this option with you, even as far as agreeing floor and office layout in order to provide a fully costed proposal to you.

If you choose to go along this route, you may gain the advantage of a perfectly adapted building to your business and, if the plot of land resides in a grant-assisted area, then the cost of plant, machinery and initial telecommunications may be the subject of a grant.

If you are in a position to purchase the building, the normal commercial terms and the basis of negotiation applies. It is certainly possible to lease a design and build property, but the developer will insist upon a minimum lease period of at least 15 years.

Business centres

Perhaps one of the most attractive options when selecting business premises is, in fact, the business or technology centre. These have been created in the last 10 years in order to promote the growth of small to medium enterprises in the UK. They consist of a single-staffed reception area, a communal meeting area available on pay-by-book basis, and the rental of a number of small offices

> One of the most attractive options is the business centre.

or commercial units. You may rent one or more units within the centre and expand your business on a pay-as-you-go basis. This represents the ultimate in flexibility and can be a very attractive option for any fast-growing business. The receptionist will answer your incoming calls in the correct way and provide a secretarial service if you require.

As a point to note, these units appear to be relatively expensive at the point of entry, but obviously can deliver significant savings over a period of time.

preparing the business

Virtual businesses

In reviewing and forecasting your space requirements for your proposed building, we are now going to suggest that you consider your business's use of technology.

The sort of technology we are talking about is listed below:

- pagers and mobile phones/computing
- telecommunication call re-routing
- the use of external call centres and helpdesks
- the use of the Internet and e-mail
- the practice of 'hot desking', where individuals use desks on a first-come-first-served basis, performing most of their work either from home, the car or customer's premises.

> Your business may ultimately be considered as a 'virtual business'.

This technology we will leave you to investigate at your own pace. Some of the above we mention in greater detail in Chapter 8: 'Staying afloat' and again in Chapter 11: Effective use of technology'. At this stage, it is enough to know that the practices listed above allow you as a business to operate from far smaller and more flexible premises than has historically been the case.

Take the position of renting part of a business centre, and your business could, in fact, simply make use of the secretarial and meeting room functions without renting further office space. This will allow you the efficient use of telecommunications and mobile computing to work from home on most occasions, whilst having the benefits of a physical office on a pay-as-you use-basis. Your business may therefore ultimately be considered as a 'virtual business'.

'Imagination is more important than knowledge.' – Einstein

Seed-bed and nursery units

The last 3 years have seen the rise, through universities, TECs and private investors, of the business nursery or seed-bed units. These consist of single-room offices and maybe further operational space. Mentors are on hand who offer advice and guide you through the 'business viable' barrier. Seek out these centres if you have a technology-based idea and wish to set up a business which requires funding and support to get it going.

LEASE, RENT OR BUY?

Lease, rent or buy – the most obvious questions to ask when considering these three options does, in fact, relate to the strength of your balance sheet. If you have been trading for a relatively short time or your net asset position is not particularly high, the cash contained within your business must be clearly focused as operating capital.

Operating capital is the lifeblood of your business and must never be reduced in pursuit of fixed assets.

The choice in this instance must exclude the purchasing of property due to the minimum 20 per cent deposit required to match an 80 per cent commercial mortgage.

The number of properties available on the market on a pure rental basis are few and far between once you get over 1000 square feet. Business owners are therefore driven along the road to leasing a building for a number of years. There are a great number of pitfalls associated with leasing arrangements, which we will be describing in detail in the following section. Our advice, however, does not replace that of a good solicitor, and we will simply provide information that will enable you to focus your instructions to your solicitor and, of course, will save you money.

Buy

If your business has been trading for a sufficient period of time, to enable you to build retained earnings or cash reserves, you may decide to embark on the purchasing route.

There are many ways of purchasing business premises, but one of the most effective ways that we know of is to use your personal self-administered pension scheme to own the property. This effectively means that your pension owns the commercial building and charges your business a commercial rent on an annual basis. You can therefore see that your business can fund your pension in a very tax-efficient way by renting to you the commercial premises that you may otherwise have purchased.

Our advice to you now is to seek out a good tax accountant who is comfortable with these types of transactions.

Lease

On the subject of leases, we will give you some of the opportunities and pit-falls associated with leasing which we experienced and think important to detail.

The first point to consider is the length of the lease in terms of years. If the lease is written within the 1954 Rent Act, then as a tenant you have certain rights of continuance when the terms of the lease come to an end. If, how-ever, the lease is written outside the 1954 Rent Act, you have *no rights of continuance*, and the landlord may insist that you vacate the premises by the stated date.

> **Tip 1**: *Our advice to you is not to accept a long lease term, as your circumstances will certainly change over time.*

Our experiences with our retail outlet were that we naively accepted a 15-year term of lease in a new building with a start-up business in an uncertain economic climate. As we plunged into recession in 1990 and closed the shop, supposedly stemming our losses, we found ourselves personally liable for a further 14 years of rental and service charge payments, which averaged £8000 per year.

We had no legal basis for contending these circumstances and were forced to negotiate our release from these terms. Fortunately, we were successful but only by proposing to sublease our unit to a third party, which would have not been in keeping with the arcade's image. However, it is not normal for leases to be cancelled and had we not identified specific circumstances, we would have certainly been liable for the full £112 000.

If you are a new business, or have a short trading history, then you will almost certainly be asked to give directors' or personal guarantees. *Our advice is simple. Try to avoid this at all costs*. If it becomes the only option, and you have negotiated hard, be aware of the liability that could arise to you per-sonally. Don't be bullied into accepting that guarantees are normal and nec-essary for the lease to be completed.

> **Tip 2**: *Beware of the rent review.*

This usually manifests as an innocent little clause which gives the landlord the rights to review his rent (rarely downwards) to account for prevailing market conditions. This, in effect, gives the landlord the right to increase your rent and service charge by as much as he thinks he can get away with.

You must seek to define a percentage by which the rent may increase, pre-agree the rent over the entire term, or to reduce the frequency of rent reviews to zero if at all possible.

> ### Tip 3: Understand the break clauses.

This is the set of circumstances that allows you or your landlord to break the contract and either vacate or be vacated from the premises. From the landlord's point of view, this is usually associated with non-payment of rent, service charge or other bills, as well as an onerous list of 'thou shalt not' associated with the business and its activities.

In all of the above matters, you must seek to *lengthen the notice period* which the landlord must serve upon you in order to protect your business.

In the case of your own break clauses, you must seek to *shorten time periods* in order to give yourself as much financial flexibility as possible.

> ### Tip 4: Understand fully insured and repairing leases

This means that as a tenant you are responsible for the upkeep of the building itself (in relative portions if you are one of a number of tenants). It may seem unlikely, at the point of signing the lease, that you may find yourself covering the bill for the replacement of the lift within the building, but you must be aware of this and other potential liabilities.

Your competent solicitor will, of course, guide you through all of the stages mentioned above. Do not be pressured into signing a document that you do not consider good for your business.

> ### Tip 5: There is no such thing as a standard contract and everything is negotiable.

Before we go on to talk about the rent itself, we must point out a serious exposure relating to the year 2000. A fully insured and repairing lease tenant

preparing the business

47

will be wholly responsible in proportional terms for the replacement and/or upgrading of the landlord's equipment, in order to become year 2000 compliant. You must ensure that this circumstance is excluded from your liability of costs, and that the landlord gives you specific written assurances that any associated costs will be born solely by him/her.

As a matter of good practice, all landlords should be prepared to give assurances of the building's compliance with the year 2000 and should state so clearly.

Rent and service charge

The charges applicable to a leasing contract usually take two forms, mainly the rent and the service charge. Rent, being fairly self-explanatory, is usually portrayed as a 'pound per sq. ft' figure. The service charge, however, is a cost levied in support of the landlord's cost of maintenance, which may even extend to the gardening, repainting of the building and, in the case of retail outlets, the advertising of the arcade and the cleaning of communal areas.

It is very important as an in-going tenant that you fully understand the service charges that will be levied. If you are unsure, seek written clarification as in our experiences, the service charge is often a means to the landlord's cost recovery, which is sometimes open to question. As a point of negotiation you may wish to explore the possibility of capping the service charge to limit your exposure.

The rent, however, is a perfectly negotiable figure. The negotiation must start with your own understanding of the other rental charges in the local area. It is tempered with the information as to how long the premises have been vacant and the requirements of the landlord in attracting a tenant.

Here are some negotiation statements you may like to consider in your transaction.

- The landlord grants you a rent-free period of 6 months in order to offset your moving-in costs.
- The first year's rent (thereafter) is discounted by, say, 40 per cent.
- The second year's rent is also subject to discount and then reverts to normal.
- The normal rent is fully negotiable even after the acceptance of the above.

Business insurance

You should be aware that the insurance premium that you pay in respect of risk of theft, health and safety, public liability and general contents insurance will vary from postcode to postcode. Each building that you view, therefore, may have a different insurance premium attached to it. In addition, the safeguards that an insurer will insist upon, such as barred windows, for example, need to be considered as an expenditure item before you make your final selection.

> *Tip 6:* *Ask your insurance broker to visit your shortlisted premises and provide a written quotation in respect of each building. This must also include mandatory security measures that you will then have to cost. This service will be provided free by your insurance broker.*

Crime rates

Clearly, there are areas within certain towns and cities that are considered to be a higher risk in terms of theft and vandalism than others. Your insurance broker will certainly have a view on which areas these are, but a free-of-charge service is also provided by the police crime prevention officers. It can be particularly damaging to a business, both in financial as well as morale terms, to experience frequent acts of crime against your business property, cars or employees.

> *Tip 7:* *Obtain a free report detailing crime rates for each building you have shortlisted.*

Financial assistance

The forms of financial assistance are constantly changing but we have endeavoured to suggest just a few contacts that you may like to make when exploring this subject.

In areas where the primary industry has substantially declined, such as coal mining and textile areas, you will find these becoming 'designated areas'. The European Union will make funds available in the pursuit of jobs and wealth creation in these areas. Similarly, the UK government, through local government offices, the Training Enterprise Councils (TEC) and the local councils, may also offer assistance.

In certain areas, the exiting primary industry has often made funds available in support of businesses. One of these was the British Coal Enterprise Fund, which until recently has been offering capital support to job-creating businesses.

The key phrase here, of course, as we have now mentioned, is *job creation*.

The offer of grants or support funding will rely upon the fact that you are either creating new jobs, or indeed safeguarding existing jobs. If this is demonstrably the case, the TEC may provide employee-training grants or offer an amount per employee, based on agreed criteria.

The local council may also provide assistance in pursuit of jobs within certain city boundaries.

In our computer services company, we were considering, at one stage, moving across the county border, but were persuaded to stay within our existing area by the local council who offered us a £10 000 grant in support of our relocation costs and retention of 30 jobs within their area.

The government's prolific use of urban regeneration programmes has led to certain areas within cities and counties being designated as enterprise zones. This can give rise to many benefits to small businesses, taking the form of zero or discounted business rates, subsidised rentals, support teams and other 'sweeteners'.

Our advice to you in search for grant assistance is to:

- talk to your business link who will provide grant search assistance
- discuss your business with the local council's economic development team
- expand your geographic search area to take account of enterprise zones in your county.

PRACTICAL STEPS

- Be clear about your primary driver for relocation.

- Understand your financial boundaries.

- Get to know all properties available in the marketplace.

- Negotiate your lease terms and instruct your solicitor accordingly.

- Beware of the year 2000 liabilities.

- Check the building use restrictions carefully.

- Drive a hard bargain and *don't* feel guilty.

- Your legal costs are your own but *don't* accept the landlord's legal costs.

- Don't rush your selection and don't give personal guarantees if possible.

- Maximize your grant assistance.

preparing the business

training to stay alive

The raft

Finance and accounting

Glossary of financial terms

Sales forecasting

Organization of business

Running a board of directors

The human mind, once stretched by a new idea, never regains its original dimension. – Oliver Wendell Holmes

Before we explore this chapter in detail, let us recap for a short while to see what we have achieved. Whether you have been in business for a while or whether you are in a start-up business, you will have now completed Chapter 1, which planned your shareholders' agreement and generated your company's mission statement and goals.

> Monitor your business effectively on a daily basis.

We then continued in Chapter 2 to write a quality business plan, budget and cash-flow spreadsheets, so that you can monitor your business effectively on a daily basis. In Chapter 3 we have discussed the opportunities and pitfalls associated with business premises and the need to keep expenditure of this nature under tight control.

The emphasis of these chapters has been to encourage you to extend your entrepreneurial skills and talents in order to get the best outcome in all of your business dealings.

To get a real head start in the world of business, it is absolutely essential that you have working knowledge of finance and accounting, sales forecasting, company organization and board procedures. These are the four basic ingredients from which all good businesses are made. It does sound time-consuming, but we have tried to make it enjoyable, understandable and based on practical solutions and advice.

Before we move into these sections, we would like to share with you a model of a typical business with which we have drawn an analogy with a raft (see Fig. 4.1). We do not like the complicated theories of business structure found in many textbooks and therefore have made up a simple diagram, which will hopefully stay in your mind during the most complex of days.

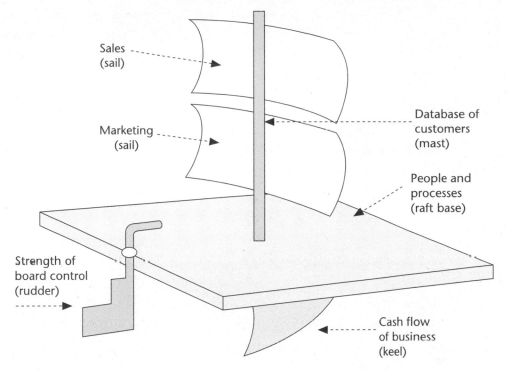

Fig 4.1 THE BUSINESS RAFT

THE RAFT

Why a raft?

Because it represents a method of transport that, if left unmanaged, is intrinsically unstable, *exactly like a company.*

Below are four questions we never want you to forget. In fact, we would like you to ask them of yourself on a once-a month-basis.

These questions are:

1 How much cash do I have at my disposal for the *running* of my business?
2 What is the level of sales this month, and what am I *realistically* projecting for next month and the month after?
3 Is the board of directors or senior management *controlling* the business, rather than simply doing the work of the business, and has a formal board meeting taken place this month?
4 Am I doing everything possible to *leverage* my opportunities to increase sales, cash and efficiencies?

If you need any help answering these questions, these four areas will be covered in greater detail later in the book. By simply focusing on these questions, you will be forced to consider the model of the company raft and all of its component parts.

■ Raft base

The construction of the raft *base* is representative of the *structure* of the company and of its *process*.

For example, it may represent a small office or set of offices, your office equipment, desks, filing cabinets, etc.; your stationery, paperwork forms and processes. If you are a services company, this may be fairly typical.

If you manufacture, it will represent all of the above, and also include the factory, the manufacturing equipment, the warehouse, lorries, etc.

If you resell a product, it may be a subset or mixture of the above scenarios.

The people who sit on the raft clearly represent you and your employees.

Now we will look at the various elements that make up the raft, then we can set sail and examine control, navigation, stability and the future of our company.

■ The keel

represents the cash in the bank or the cash available to the business.
The more cash available to the business, the deeper the keel goes. As anyone knows, having stepped into a wobbly boat, the deeper the keel, the more stable the platform. On a raft, however, as in a company, the situation is magnified. Imagine the difficulty in stepping onto a raft without a keel. One small wave and a swift introduction to the water follows!

Thus it is desirable that we raise and retain *sufficient cash* in our company in order to remain stable. We will call this cash *working capital* and will refer to it constantly in the following sections. Working capital does not have to be cash in the bank, however; it could be credit lines available from suppliers, but in the end represents a positive cash flow in the business.

■ The rudder

is the board of directors, which controls the company.
The size of the rudder is directly proportional to the skills of the individual directors, particularly the managing director, and the frequency and professionalism of the board meetings.

Thus the rudder, as the board of directors, offers direction to the raft, the impact of which is determined by the size (core skills) of the rudder (board).

■ **The mast**

represents the customer database of the company.
Without a clearly defined list of customers, which is regularly managed, maintained and added to, making sales will be very difficult indeed.

The bigger the database, the better it is managed; the higher the mast, the greater the potential.

■ **The sails**

are easy to remember as the sales of the company.
The greater the area of the canvas, the more revenue is gained. The method of selling, e.g. direct salesmen or catalogue-selling agents, etc., will be represented by the sails. The second sail refers to general marketing and niche markets. A smaller sail in square area, therefore, can move the raft just as fast as a large sail which is misaligned to the winds.

Trimming the sails, as a nautical term, can be considered in business as analyzing your marketplace, looking for market advantages, niche markets and maximum return from your sales department.

Setting sail

You have set a business plan (adjusted the rudder), opened an operational office (built the raft base), borrowed some money to match your own (set the keel), and targeted your customers with a mailshot or cold calls (hoisted the sails).

It is your company.

You are on your way. People are recruited to improve sales, manage operations, finance, engineering/production, etc., and things look good. The sails are full with orders, the database is growing. You adjust the sails slightly as any good sales manager would, and your raft picks up speed.

What happens next is up to you! After all, it is your company. Your chances of survival are now going to drop dramatically unless you take rapid and ongoing actions. More than 83 per cent of companies last less than 5 years. Will yours be one of them?

If yours is, chances are that you will have a bulging order book when you go bust. Nine out of ten companies go bust because of management failure, not lack of sales.

The management failure lies not in people management, nor sales management. It lies in the management of finance and in the strategic direction setting: the two are inextricably linked.

Cash-flow on our company raft is depicted by the keel. With unmonitored payment terms from the customers, lack of focus on debt collection, *the keel grows shorter*. The speed of the raft, coupled with a short keel, makes for a dangerously unstable platform. If allowed to continue, capsize is surely inevitable, throwing off all the employees and crashing the company.

The warning sound is formalized by the banks, who regretfully cannot extend any more overdraft, and are now looking for a repayment scheme. The directors finally take note.

In panic, they reach for the rudder, which is woefully small due to their lack of skill and frequency of meeting on a formal basis. The rudder fails to affect the raft's direction and with a sickening lurch the raft (company) smashes onto a rock (annoyed creditor) and the company is dissolved.

Staying afloat and succeeding

The previous section details an all-too-common occurrence that need never happen. Even poor cash-flow can be managed, given a large enough rudder. Do not forget, even a coracle is stable with a skilled oarsman in it.

So how do we make that rudder the right size? Remember, the rudder is synonymous with the skills of the directors, and the frequency of them formally meeting. In fact, the process of rudder enlargement is very simple.

In the previous section 'Why a raft' we identified the key areas of a company and the four key questions which we must constantly ask

To recap, here they are again.

- How much cash do I have at my disposal for the *running* of my business?
- What is the level of sales this month, and what am I *realistically* projecting for next month and the month after?
- Is the board of directors or senior management *controlling* the business, rather than simply doing the work of the business, and has a formal board meeting taken place this month?

■ Am I doing everything possible to *leverage* my opportunities to increase sales, cash and efficiencies?

We cannot direct the wind, but we can adjust the sails.

We are now going to break down the structure of the raft into the four areas defined as:

1 finance and accounting   (*keel*)
2 the structure of the company as it grows   (*the base of the raft*)
3 the sales forecasting and controls   (*the mast and sails*)
4 the board's behaviour on a collective basis. (*the rudder of the raft*)

These areas will each become the subject of a dedicated *training* module, designed to improve your knowledge in each area. Once you become competent in these subjects, sailing the raft will become much easier, and the chances of success will increase dramatically.

> **Even a coracle is stable with a skilled oarsman.**

FINANCE AND ACCOUNTING

The following training module seeks to demystify and explain clearly the standard accounting terms that you will need to understand as a business person. In our experiences, these must be understood and, if you have any further questions as a result of this training module, we urge you to seek the advice of a competent accountant.

It is true to say that if you do not understand finance and accounting, you will be unsuccessful in convincing financial institutions to lend you money and you will not allow yourself the opportunity to reach your fullest potential.

■ **Purpose** – the purpose of accounting is to 'match expenses with current revenue', to present a realistic picture of profits earned by the organization.

■ **Cost accounting** – the art of 'pricing the company's inventories' so that we can achieve the purpose outlined above.

■ **Management accounting** – the art of producing financial information in a format designed to help managers manage.

■ **Budgeting** – the art of estimating the financial requirements (income and outgoing) for a 'future period' of an operation. Then, having made these estimates, to use them as a comparative measure against the actual experience of the company as it operates through this time period.

Accounting function (people/tasks)

Chartered accountants (ACAs in the UK)

The chartered accountant's job is to match current costs with current revenues and to present an audited profit statement and balance sheet.

■ Management accountant

The management accountant's job is to help management manage. He is involved with budgeting and measuring variances between estimated and actual expenses. He designs charts of accounts and methods of presenting figures.

■ Cost accountant

The cost accountant's job is to price inventories and to establish unit cost of sales. Sometimes confused with cost estimators whose job it is to make estimates of unit costs and contract costs for good/services to be provided.

■ Financial manager/director

The financial manager's job is to manage cash, current and fixed assets, current and fixed liabilities, and to provide all necessary funds from banks, raise money in the share market, venture capital, government and private funding agencies and to evaluate investments. His job is to finance the business for the lowest capital cost and with the maximum safeguards against risks.

■ Finance controller

The controller's job is to reassure, evaluate, and report on income and outgoing activities, giving an independent assessment of the financial performance of functions. Can be an employee who authorises spending, hence 'controller'.

GLOSSARY OF FINANCIAL TERMS

These are the terms that you will find relating to the operating statement, otherwise known as the profit and loss account. These terms are explained in greater detail later in this section.

Operating statement

- Profit and loss statement: sales, income, turnover, revenue, receipts, fees earned, hence earnings
- Expense/revenue/cost accounts.
- Chart of accounts
- Direct expenses: cost of goods sold, cost of operations
- Indirect expenses: overhead elements, general administrative costs
- Depreciation

- Margins: gross operating net before; net after
- Interest
- Profit
- Taxes
- Dividends
- Retained earnings
- Fixed costs
- Variable costs
- Break even
- Standard costs.

Balance sheet

These are the terms that relate to the balance sheet and are explained in detail later in this section. Where you see numbers in brackets, please refer to the flow diagram, Fig 4.2 (page 62).

- Current assets: cash, debtors, stock
- Fixed assets
- Reserves
- Capital employed (1-2+3+4+5-6-7+8+9)
- Total assets (1-2+3+4+5)
- Current liabilities: creditors, payables
- Fixed liabilities
- Long-term debt
- Short-term debt overdraft
- Facilities
- Net worth, book value (8+9)
- Gearing/leverage (7+8/9)

- Quick ratio (3+4/6)
- Acid test ratio (3+4+5/6)
- Turn inventory / stock debtors, creditors
- Ageing of accounts
- Cash flow
- Debentures – secured or unsecured
- Shares: par value/no par value/preference
- Loan capital
- EPS, PEM (earnings per share, price earnings multiple)
- Share price

preparing the business

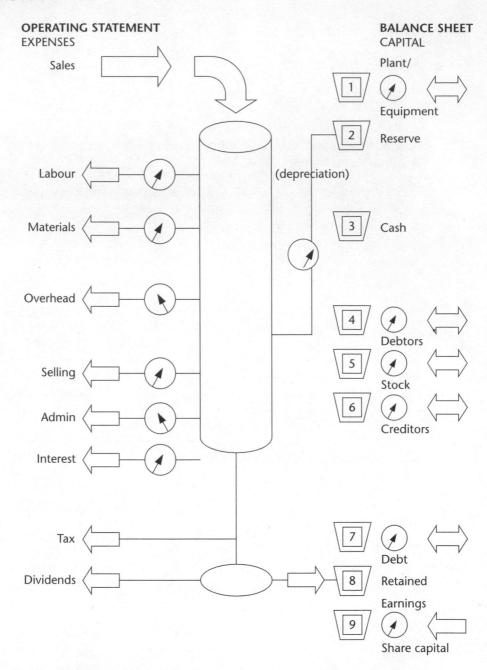

OPERATING STATEMENT
EXPENSES

Sales

Labour

Materials

Overhead

Selling

Admin

Interest

Tax

Dividends

BALANCE SHEET
CAPITAL

1   Plant/
    Equipment

2   Reserve

(depreciation)

3   Cash

4
    Debtors
5
    Stock
6
    Creditors

7
    Debt
8   Retained
    Earnings
9
    Share capital

Fig. 4.2 FLOW DIAGRAM

Cost terms

■ Fixed and variable

All operations have an element of expense related to time, and not to the work which the organization does. Rent, for example, is a charge for a period of time, not for the work being done. Such period expenses are called *fixed*. That means the volume of work does not affect them.

> All operations have an element of expense related to time.

There are other expenses which vary with the business activities. For example, materials are purchased for use in a product. As more product is produced, more materials are consumed. These costs are called *variable*.

The graph in Fig.4.3 shows the relationship between the fixed and variable costs with business activity. Overlaid on this cost graph is a line showing the relationship of income with business activity. The point where the lines cross is called the breakeven point.

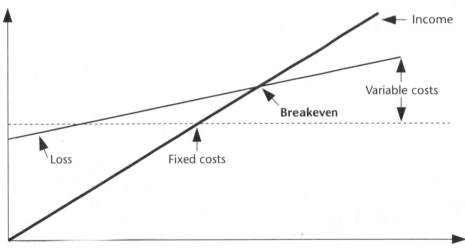

Fig. 4.3 FIXED AND VARIABLE COSTS WITH BUSINESS ACTIVITY

■ Direct and indirect

Figure 4.4 shows the background for the words 'direct', 'indirect' and 'overheads'. Those expenses directly connected to the product are called direct: labour, materials, sometimes power, supplies, etc. As the expense gets somewhat away from hands-on direct contact with the product, the expense is

called indirect. Indirect expenses can be inspection, engineering, maintenance, etc. As the indirect get more indirect, it becomes an overhead expense
item.

First-level overheads are often called factory burden or factory overhead, and
higher up they are called general and administrative expenses or general
overheads.

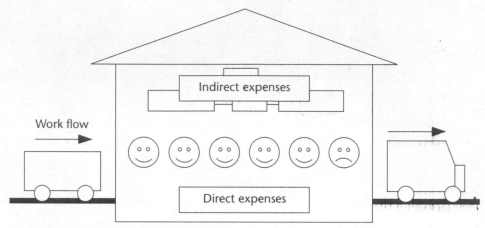

Fig. 4.4 DIRECT, INDIRECT AND OVERHEADS

Financial accounting system

The accounting system measures the flow of cash throughout the business
and interrelates this cash-flow with the outside world. It can be described as
an oil refinery, with the 'pipe still' as the operating statement and the 'tank
farm' as the balance sheet. Thus, the operating statement deals with the cash
churning in the operations and the balance sheet deals with the storage of
cash in the tanks.

Flow meters
The meters which measure the flow of cash on the operating side are equivalent to 'flow meters', which measure the rate at which the cash flows, or
flow per unit of time.

Sight gauges
The meters which measure the level of cash in the tanks are equivalent to
'sight gauges' or liquid level gauges, which measure the level in the tank at
a given point in time.

The holes drilled along the pipe still, through which cash flows, are called accounts. There must be at least one pipe coming in at the top, at least one pipe coming off the side, and at least one pipe coming off the bottom. Other than that the holes drilled on the operating side can be of any number and at any location. The key, however, is to make sure that each pipe is labelled and that all who use it know what is flowing through it.

View glasses are drilled at any place along the column, through which one can look to see what is passing by at that point. These too can be located at any place along the pipe and can be as many as one would like. What passes by at these locations represent margins or contributions toward what happens further down the pipe still. (*See* Fig. 4.4.)

It is a practice to place the more direct expenses near the top and the more indirect toward the bottom. The only connection between the operating statement and the balance sheet is through the reserve – depreciation pipeline(s) and the retention of earnings pipeline.

The 'chart of accounts' is a book containing the names given to each pipe (code numbers as well), plus a description of what expense elements flow through each pipe.

These code numbers are called 'nominal codes'. They are usually four-digit numbers and allow us to map the measurement of the key events in a standard way.

The name 'expenses' is given to the cash flowing through the operating side, while 'capital' is the word given to the cash on the balance sheet side.

The system is in constant motion, 24 hours a day. But accountants only read the meters once in a while: monthly, quarterly, semi-annually, or annually. These measures, therefore, apply only at that point in time when the meters were actually read. The flow meters tell what has gone through the pipes during the period between readings, and the sight gauges tell what the level was in the tank at that particular moment in time. They do not tell what it was a few minutes before or after.

Figure 4.2 should be kept in front of the manager whenever he talks with an accountant.

Depreciation

Although there are some people who actually write off all of their capital spending in the year the machine or plant was acquired, most people do not.

It is believed that plant and equipment (usually items costing over £100) will have a life expectancy greater than 1 year, and therefore only a part of the purchase price should be written off in any one year. This practice is believed to more accurately 'match current expenses with current income'.

An example

If a piece of equipment cost £1000 and is thought to have a life of 10 years, it is the practice to write off one-tenth of the original purchase each year over a 10-year period.

Year 1 The XYZ machine is purchased for £1000.

During year 1, it is the practice to write off half of the first year's depreciation rather than try to pro-rata, by months, the actual usage in the first year.

Year 2 The depreciation would be £100; year 3 yet another £100 through to year 10, by which time the entire amount of £1000 would have been written off. By writing off £100 per year, over the 10 years the original £1000 will have been recovered and retained in a tank called' reserve for depreciation'.

The pro-rata write-off of any expense is called setting up a 'reserve'.

> **Capital invested can be written off at different rates.**

When the same amount is written off each year, this method is called 'straight line depreciation'.

There are other variations to this straight line theme. Capital invested can be written off at different rates, with most of it being written off in the early years and less later on. These non-linear rates of write-off all have their own names and mathematical formulas but in no case can more be written off than was originally paid out.

This gives rise to the argument that 'in times of inflation, the writing-off of only the original cost does not provide enough reserve to replace the item when it becomes worn out'. This suggests that more should be written off than was originally paid, in order to recover a larger sum required to purchase, in the future, the same machine predicted to be at a higher price. This theory is called 'inflation accounting', i.e. providing enough reserve to allow for inflation.

Balance sheet ratios

■ Cash

A company needs to have a cash balance to meet day-to-day needs. This ranges from a high of 4 per cent on sales to a low of ½ per cent on sales. For those companies where cash is managed by a central operation (at group level), the cash ratio can be slightly negative. And of course where a company continues to operate with an overdraft facility (negotiated with the bank), then it too will be negative. But, on balance, a 1 per cent cash level to sales should be sound and workable.

■ Debtors

The debtor's ratio to sales depends on the speed of payment by the company's customer. The company's own credit terms affect this ratio and the effectiveness of their credit controls has yet another effect.

If all the customers pay within 1 month of invoice or receipt of goods/services, at any one time, there will be 1 month of sales outstanding. The ratio would be 1/12th which = 8.3 per cent on sales.

If all customers are slow and pay their invoices in 2 months, the ratio would be 1/6 which = 16.6 per cent on sales.

By taking the actual level of debtors from the company's balance sheet and by dividing this number by the sales figure, it is easy to calculate the ratio as it is being experienced. Then by multiplying this ratio times 365 days in the year, one can compute instantly the average length of time it takes for the customers to pay. Some will pay sooner and some longer but, on average, you will have the accurate number of days.

In planning the company's financial future, it is useful to effect improvements in this ratio, then each year should have a different ratio with which to compute the balance sheet accounts.

■ Creditors

This ratio depends on the company's willingness to pay their own creditors and, as such, is almost completely within the control of the company. Hence this ratio can be set most accurately. It is, in part, influenced by trade practices, but even so it can be negotiated from a very short period of time to a very long period of time.

> *As a small business, the extended use of credit lines from your suppliers can be a very inexpensive way of borrowing money and therefore, as a golden rule, your creditor ratio should always exceed your debtor ratio.*

preparing the business

If the company takes 90 days to pay for the purchases of goods or services, the ratio of creditors to *purchases* is 90/365 or 24.65 per cent. Then, to put this ratio on to a sales base, one must multiply this ratio by the percentage of purchases there are to sales. If these purchases to sales run at 30 per cent, the ratio on sales would be 0.30 x 24.65, or 7.40 per cent on sales.

Again, by taking actual creditor figures off the balance sheet, and dividing this number directly by the sales figure one calculates immediately this ratio, which can then be adjusted one way or another.

■ Stock

The turn of stock is the number of times the stock level (sterling value) goes into the annual sales level. If sales are £100 and the stock is £10, the stock turn is 100/10 or 10 times. That means there is 1/10th of a year's stock on hand at any point in time, or 36.5 days of stock. Stock, as a percentage of sales, is the stock level divided by sales, which in the case above is 10 per cent. The reciprocal of the turn is the same as a percentage on sales.

All other balance sheet items, which vary directly with sales, can be computed using the nominal account to the level of sales. In every case, the ratio has a characteristic which is unique to the operation being planned.

These ratios are extremely accurate and reliable. The total capital required for any business can be easily calculated. It is a simple matter to develop a programme for financing any operation.

■ Plant and equipment

There is a relationship between sales and the capital invested in fixed assets (buildings/plant/equipment). This relationship tends to be common within a given industry such as printing, where there is a standard relationship from which few vary.

In practice, if one company hires plant and equipment or leases it, the value for these assets do *not* appear on the balance sheet. The ratio between sales and assets for such a company would not look like its industrial sisters'. Such variations in ratios must be understood, but do not mitigate against their use as they are powerful tools for planning in the face of uncertainty.

By dividing the sales figure by the capital invested in plant and equipment, it is possible to establish what the capital required will be when the plant doubles in business: namely, it will double. One must take a look at capacity considerations and shift considerations before jumping to that conclusion but, on balance, as a business grows so does the need for capital support in the fixed assets of the business.

This relationship can be used to one's advantage, as it has been found that a company will grow proportionately to the plough-back of capital into its assets. Some companies will grow faster and others will grow slower. Those who grow faster may be bleeding the company and will ultimately pay for this omission and those who grow slower may be over-capitalizing their activities with non-business generating investments.

> **Some companies will grow faster and others will grow slower.**

The definition of 'plough-back': the annual capital investment divided by the amount of annual depreciation being written off. If the same amount of investment is being reinvested as is being written off, a 100 per cent plough-back would result. A 100 per cent plough-back should support a 10 per cent growth rate.

■ Acid test

The acid test ratio is cash plus debtors plus stock divided by creditors. This will give you a number which in all cases should be greater than 1 to maintain a solvent position. If this figure is below 1, refer to 'Running a board of directors' later in this chapter.

■ Quick ratio

Cash plus debtors divided by creditors. This ratio indicates the liquidity of the business, which again should be above 1 at all times.

In many small and growing businesses, you will find the quick ratio often falling below 1. When this happens, there is insufficient cash available to the business, which increases the trading risk significantly. For more information on how to address this situation, refer to Chapter 8: 'Staying afloat'.

■ Gearing

This is a ratio that is expressed as total debt divided by the sum of retained earnings plus share capital. This figure is usually seen between 5 and 40 per cent for larger, more stable companies who have been trading for some time. In small businesses, however, figures in excess of 200 per cent have been known, although at this stage the lending institutions become very nervous. The expression 'gearing', is essentially the ability of the company to repay or cover its debts.

SALES FORECASTING

A winner is someone who sets his goals, commits himself to those goals, and then pursues his goals with all the ability given to him.

In this section we will examine two parts to the sales forecasting process. The first is the annual budget, and the second is the monthly prediction for the following month's sales, in order to plan the operations of the business.

In our experience, the sales budgeting process is one that gives rise to huge variations between the planned performance and the actual performance in the business. Every year, we used to plan as scientifically as possible, and project these wonderful figures that seemed every year to be wholly achievable. Each year, something would happen that would, in retrospect, commit our original figures to the annals of fiction rather than fact.

> Plan for the expansion that you seek.

The budgeting process, in a small business, becomes one of banding. It is important to plan for the expansion that you seek, and the likely resources that you will need to facilitate this growth. On the other hand, it is also important to plan for the zero growth scenario, and maybe one in-between as well. This way, you will end up with three plans, but at least you will have planned.

So, just how do you approach the annual sales forecast, and what tricks can you use to make things easier?

We will now understand the term *base business* , for this is the business that you can see as coming into the company regardless of what you do. If you have a turnover of £500 000 in the previous year, this is your base reference point. Now, what happens if you did no development work, did not expand the range of services that you offer, and simply tried to replicate what you did last year? This base business would fall away quite quickly. Your turnover at the end of this next year would probably be in the region of £300 000, maybe even less. This is shown in Fig. 4.5 as the decline curve, and please do not underestimate its steepness.

So what do we do next? Well, it is considered good practice to identify on a case-by-case basis where the development of your company is coming from. This is termed *development business* and must be considered separately from the main plan of base business.

Even if your plan is to hire more sales staff in order to increase market share and increase sales, you should identify this as a separate plan, and call it development. By using this base plus development planning method, we found that we subjected ourselves to a greater scrutiny than we would otherwise have done, and we recommend it to you.

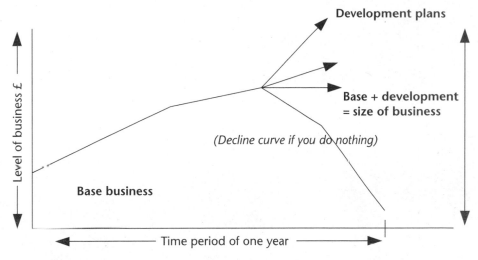

Fig. 4.5 DECLINE CURVE

The main difficulty in planning accurately within a small business is that you won't have been in business for very long, and the historical data from which you might make certain assumptions is less than reliable.

Also, the entrepreneurial manoeuvres that you will make during the course of the year may distort the data for future years. Your business is unlikely to be able to measure its market share, and so this important statistic is not available to you; so just what do you base your numbers on?

Below are some ideas that you may wish to adopt in the process of planning your top line, or your sales revenue line during the annual budgeting.

■ Use any historical data that you may have at your disposal and extrapolate.

■ Look at individual customers, and even ask them what level of spend that they anticipate with you next year. This can be a valuable insight as to the state of the relationship that you have with your customer. If the level decreases from last year, for example, you have an early opportunity to visit them to ask why. If the customer becomes cagey with you, sound the alarm bells and make a quick appointment with your contact. They may surprise you and, based upon your excellent service, tell you of a planned increase in business with your company next year.

■ If you can approach as many as 80 per cent of your major clients, the forecast for your base business can start to assume some accuracy.

■ Assume some loss of business, or the non-repeat of certain key contracts that you fulfilled last year. Don't kid yourself that Santa comes twice a year!

■ Balance your forecast against the prevalent market conditions. If the world market is in gross price decline, like, for instance, in the computer marketplace, be aware that you will have to make more sales to achieve the same level of turnover as last year.

> **Balance your forecast against the prevalent market conditions.**

■ Once you have performed all of the above on a scientific basis, apply your 'gut feel' factor to the plan. Can you really make the numbers? Don't fool yourself, you are kidding nobody except yourself.

■ If you are using the format of the spreadsheet, beware using the extrapolation function, whereby you click on the cell, and drag the value (or, even worse, the formula for increase) across the entire 12 months.

■ Each year has a holiday season, end of year, market blips for no reason, and so you must adjust your sales line for these conditions. It is easy to say that August won't be as bad this year as last, but unless you sell deckchairs or air-conditioning units, the August holiday season, and others besides, will have a negative effect, and you must recognize it.

■ If you are hiring new sales staff, allow a 3-month ramp up to an acceptable sales performance. This way your expectations will be met, as opposed to an unrealistic expectation that puts undue pressure on all staff.

Once you have planned your sales lines, you can budget for the operational overheads of the business using the spreadsheet on the diskette [■ Planning.xls].

Remember – nothing happens until you make a sale.

Now we would like to move on to talk about the monthly forecast of sales that we would encourage you to perform each and every month as a discipline. By performing this assessment, you achieve the following:

- you understand how your business is faring by comparing to the annual sales budgets
- you can more accurately plan for extra or less staff depending upon real numbers
- you send a message to your staff as to the importance of selling, and the dependence upon the customer
- you show the sales team that there is no hiding place from your understanding and scrutiny.

We will talk more about how to control a sales force in Chapter 5, but we will now see the different ways in which you can quickly assess your likely sales performance in the coming months.

The monthly forecast is particularly difficult, as we often found that we were on the opposite side of the fence to our sales staff. Their motivators in life were to portray high performance (regardless of whether this were true or not), protect their own jobs, and therefore to blame everyone but themselves if things did not go according to plan.

Now, perhaps we are being a little harsh, but in our rapidly growing business it certainly seemed that way at times. We found that we had to be very clinical about the way in which we assessed the likelihood of a deal becoming real. Once we knew this factor, we could reasonably predict the following month's sales level.

Our difficulty arose when we employed sales managers to manage the sales force. We found some of the same factors portrayed, to a lesser extent perhaps, but there were few months that went by when the measured sales were within even 10 per cent of the previous month's forecast.

So, how do you go about planning the next month's sales level?

Here is a list of measures that are crucial in order to develop a methodology by which to plan.

> - *List all quotes sent out and considered 'live'.*
> - *List all deals that are believed to be close-able for the next month.*
> - *Test the assumption for each deal by using the questions below.*

preparing the business

Here are the ten questions to ask yourself or your salesman, before accepting it as a qualified deal for next month's sales. *You must score 80 points or more.*

1 Do you know for sure that you talking to the decision-maker?   (10 points)
2 Does your customer have budget for spend already approved?   (10 points)
3 Do you know who your competition is?   (10 points)
4 Has your customer received a written quote from you?   (10 points)
5 Do you have free access to the directors of your customer?   (10 points)
6 Do you have a diarized 'close' meeting set up yet?   (10 points)
7 Have you done business with this customer before?   (10 points)
8 Has the customer given you feedback from your proposal?   (10 points)
9 Do you know on what criteria your customer will select suppliers? (10 points)
10 Have you handled all of the customer's objections yet?   (10 points)

> **Remember that selling is an art form.**

Tough list, but unless your sales approach has tackled all of the above issues, you are operating a hit-and-miss sales force, and the results will be gained on luck and not on forecasting and professionalism.

A good sales course for all front-end operatives, regardless of whether they are deemed sales staff or not, may just be your best investment if the sales skills are not your strong point.

Remember that selling is an art form, and has skills that can be learned to good effect. The art of selling is to serve your customer the best way that suits him, and therefore retaining his custom for many years.

It can take months to find a new customer, but only seconds to lose one.

We have now covered the basics of sales forecasting, which is a vital part of understanding how the raft fits together. The forecasted sales will have a knock-on effect upon the amount of cash required in the business, and the accurate prediction of sales will give more understanding and therefore power to the board of directors. It will enable them to make more informed decisions about the direction of the business, and increase the chances of success.

Before we look at the board of directors, we will now examine the structure of the business in terms of the people control, who reports to whom, and how to get the most out of your people and processes simply by organizing them effectively.

ORGANIZATION OF BUSINESS

The typical small business starts life with one or maybe two entrepreneurs in control. In the early days of the business, the entrepreneur will have total control and knowledge in all areas of the daily operation. It is true that all entrepreneurs wear many hats in these early days.

If you have been in business for a length of time, you will certainly recognize the following scenario. You are the entrepreneur and leader and have absolute control over the daily functions of the business. This control emanates from extremely detailed knowledge of customer letters, quotations, purchase orders, different suppliers, discount by product type, finance and accounting, down to the exact bank balance on a daily basis. This is your world and you live and breathe your business.

> **All entrepreneurs wear many hats.**

As your business becomes more successful, however, and the number of employees increases to around ten people, then you will gradually lose knowledge of the detail of all of these functions. It is impossible in a growth situation for you to keep ten juggling balls in the air, without eventually dropping one. There may be, for example, employees within your business who are quite able and willing to look after at least one of those juggling balls for you. There will come a time when you have to delegate work and devolve responsibility to the employees within the business.

It is extremely important at this stage to structure your organization correctly in order to follow a controlled growth path.

Failure to organize your business as the number of employees increases will lead to blockage and frustration and ultimately loss of profit to the business.

In our own company, we started as two people working from our house: the spare bedroom was our stockroom, the hallway was the clean and test area, the kitchen became 'goods out' and the garage was converted to create the office space. Between the two of us, we covered all the functions of the business from receptionist to salesman, to engineer, to packer and to transportation.

As our business became more successful, we relocated to a small industrial unit and the number of employees grew to 14 by the end of year 3. It was the hardest thing in the world for us to delegate tasks, let alone devolve responsibilities to our employees, after being used to absolute knowledge of every event for the previous 2 years.

preparing the business

In appointing management for the first time, we struggled with the question of whether we should we promote within, regardless of competence, or hire ready-trained professionals from the outside.

We took the decision to promote from within, because of our overwhelming desire for loyalty from our employees at this stage. In the computer industry this was particularly important because job flitting was very common and would obviously be costly to the business.

Looking back, we recognize with hindsight that some of our key appointments should have been made from outside the business, rather than spending incredible amounts of time overseeing and training individuals to become managers.

This decision was definitely a growth inhibitor of our business and, because of this, we would like to demonstrate some of the pros and cons of hiring decisions in Table 4.1.

Table 4.1

Internal promotion	*vs*	External hire
■ No cost of recruitment		■ Cost recovered by higher performance
■ Needs constant training		■ Already trained and can bring fresh ideas
■ Intimate knowledge of business		■ Knowledge of other businesses which could benefit yours
■ High loyalty factor		■ Avoids over-promotion internally
■ Sends a positive message to rest of staff		■ Fewer referrals for daily decisions

Clearly, the choice must remain with the business entrepreneur as to which route is taken but, having made this decision, it is worth reflecting upon the question:

■ When do you devolve responsibility and initiate a structure?

Ask yourself the following questions:
■ Do you find it difficult to retain the detail within the day-to-day running of your business?
■ Can you take a 5-day consecutive holiday without the business being affected?
■ Are your employees requesting more responsibility?

If you answer the above questions with *yes*, *no*, *yes*, the time is definitely right to consider structuring your organization immediately.

In our experience, there are two vital areas of business that the entrepreneur must not be tempted to relieve himself from the responsibility of.

These are:

- **Sales performance and customer relationships**
- **The daily cash position of the business.**

See Chapter 5: 'Sales and marketing strategies', for tips on the leader's responsibility for sales.

> **Focus the key operational areas into functional business units.**

During the growth cycle of our own business, we resolved most of our operational and organizational difficulties by adopting standard industry models for the organization of businesses. These are shown below. The importance of a good organizational structure within the business is to focus the key operational areas into functional business units.

For a simple start-up structure that is valid for most businesses, please see Figure 4.6.

■ **The small business under £10 million**

Fig. 4.6 THE SMALL BUSINESS

Refer to the organizational design rules for guidance and tips on how to structure your business correctly found on page (81).

■ **The expansion phase – the operational and development stages**

As your business grows, you will find your opportunities for entering new markets or developing new products will necessitate what we call development work. This may be seen in terms of market research, technical development, capital investment analysis or expansion by acquisition.

preparing the business

This function normally falls to the managing director in a small business as part of his function. But, it is important to recognize this business development function as a separate entity and not just simply part of the managing director's job.

Whilst all this development work has to be performed, there is still the question of daily survival in terms of sales fulfilment, engineering/manufacturing. We will now refer to these functions as the operations of the business. Eventually, the split of work will require a senior appointment within the business to manage the operations and the characteristics of this individual and the way in which they are measured and rewarded differ from that of the development function. This is simply explained in Fig.4.7.

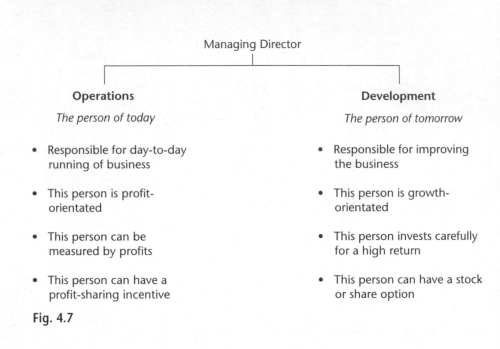

Managing Director

Operations	**Development**
The person of today	*The person of tomorrow*
• Responsible for day-to-day running of business	• Responsible for improving the business
• This person is profit-orientated	• This person is growth-orientated
• This person can be measured by profits	• This person invests carefully for a high return
• This person can have a profit-sharing incentive	• This person can have a stock or share option

Fig. 4.7

■ Medium-sized company: £10 to £30 million turnover

> The title of director or manager is very emotive and irreversible.

Using Fig. 4.7, we can now see how this reflects in the medium-sized organization (Figure 4.8)

So far, we have described the function within the business, such as sales, finance, etc., but we have not defined the seniority of the individual who should be heading up this function. This can be as just as important as getting the framework organization correct, as the title of director or manager is a very emotive and irreversible step to take.

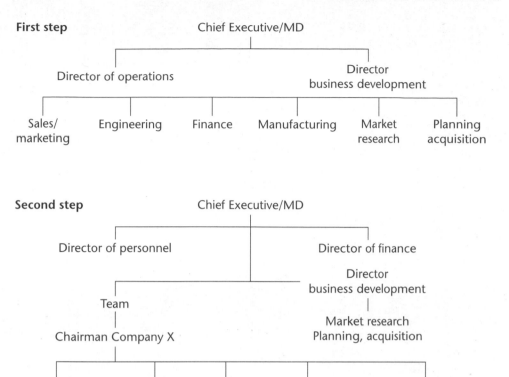

Fig. 4.8 THE MEDIUM-SIZED COMPANY

To help you to take these crucial steps, we have devised a simple method that you can use in order to formulate your approach to the individual functions.

The managing director's contribution

During this time of change, and the move to a more structured organization, the entrepreneur or managing director can experience confusion in where the prime focus, the business, should be as the business develops.

To help you identify the primary contribution of the managing director, we have devised a summary linked to the phases of development of your business.

Table 4.2 was a table that we referred to constantly during the developing cycles of our business, and, although the turnover phasing may not directly relate to your business, the right-hand column will certainly describe the managing director's development curve.

Table 4.2
THE DEVELOPMENT OF THE MANAGING DIRECTOR

Phases of development	Functional emphasis	M.D.'s contribution
Start-up phase £350 000 critical point (0–3 years)	Accounting Purchasing Management training Technical service: • engineering • customer Quality control Budgeting	Extreme personal energy/enthusiasm Skills required in: • selling • accounting
£1 050 000 survival point (3–5 years)	Departmental planning Sales and marketing	Planning skills and willingness to plan
£1 750 000 business point	Business planning Incentives Productivity Market development	Managing development skills Willingness to coach
Growth phase £4 900 000 systems and logistics point	Product development Market research	Investment analysis skills
£7 000 000 organization point – divisionalization	Diversification	Strategic planning skills
Consolidation and extension phase £21 000 000 international point	Legal and accounting Acquisition Outside consultants Outside specialists	Sociology and communication skills
Economic size limit £112 000 000 decentralization point	Public ownership Shareholder and financial institution relations	Single scenario strategy
Business farming Unlimited size Point of pluralism	Holding company function Strategic management: • Keep or sell • Make or buy	Government relations skills: lobby, politics Institution relations: finance, cultural, educational, political

Function analysis chart

Table 4.3 lists the majority of the functions prevalent to a typical business. If the terminology is not right for your business, adapt it, but there is a copy on the diskette for you to use called [■ **Function Analysis.doc**].

The columns 1,2, and 3 relate to how critical the function is to the business or its contribution to positive cash-flow. Taking 1 as the most critical and 3 as the least critical, place a cross in the column next to the function. Once you have completed this chart, turn the chart 90 degrees to the left so that the columns are to the top of the page. All of the functions highlighted in column 1 should be assigned to the daily job description of a director. Column 2 should be assigned to the daily job description of a manager and column 3 to the operatives within the business.

So far in this section, we have identified the organizational pressures of the entrepreneur in an expanding business. We have shown some organizational models that you can adopt along with some help defining the importance of each function within the organization.

As a final part in this section, we would like to list some golden rules for organizational design to ensure you have some appropriate guidelines and measures to follow.

ORGANIZATIONAL DESIGN RULES

1 Gather together 'like work' and assign a single manager (like work – one boss).
2 Do not let one-over-one management authority relationships exist, such as the chairman and managing director followed by the deputy chairman and managing director followed by managing director and deputy managing director.

> Separate development activities from operational activities

3 Span of control should be set between 3 and 7 at management levels and between 15 and 35 at worker levels.
4 Avoid, at all costs, a matrix organization. Even when brand management is involved, make sure that the cross-over manager is there for a limited time and that his end date is made known.
5 Separate the development activities of the business from the operational activities. Make sure that the development aspect of each line job is removed from the line executive's responsibility and placed in the

preparing the business

Table 4.3
FUNCTIONAL ANALYSIS CHART

Business development	3	2	1
Market research			
Product development			
Business planning			
Sales and marketing			
Field sales			
Sales order (project control) administration			
Direct mail sales			
Sales training			
Sales statistics			
Advertising and promotion			
Engineering and service			
Proposal and estimating			
Customer technical service			
Engineering design			
Customer product/field service			
Operations			
Purchasing			
Production planning and inventory control			
Assembly and test			
Quality control			
Value engineering			
Shipping			
Industrial relations			
Personnel recruiting and training			
Management development			
Wage and salary administration			
Labour relations			
Accounting and finance			
Credit			
Debtors/creditors			
Computer operations			
Tax administration			
Legal administration			
Pricing			
Leasing and financing			
Audit			
Budgeting and management accounting			
Cash and banking relations			

development activity. For example, pull out such functions as market research from marketing and assign that to the development manager, as would be R & D from engineering, and equipment and process engineering from manufacturing, as would budgeting and capital investment work be removed from accounting.

6 Do not automatically centralize functions such as corporate planning, accounting, personnel, maintenance, budgeting, purchasing, computer operations. These are all elements of the individual line manager's job who should retain these tasks for personal development. Especially, avoid the title Director of Administration or Office Manager. Do not centralize administrative activities.

7 Lift functions higher in the organization closer to the chief executive to give the function more importance. Push down those functions of lesser importance to lower reporting levels within the organization. 'Importance' is measured by how critical the activity is to the positive cash-flow of the business.

8 'Heart rule'. Do not subcontract the technical heart of the product, nor those work elements or functions which are key to the product's function.

9 Do not relinquish responsibility of daily sales or business cash-flow from the MD's prime role.

RUNNING A BOARD OF DIRECTORS

This chapter refers to a board of directors, which implies that it is only relevant to those of you who are running limited companies. If you are running partnerships, however, we still urge you to read and adopt the principles of this section, substituting the 'partner' for 'director'.

In this section we will explore the relationships between shareholders and directors and dispel the myths about the roles and rights of the shareholders and directors within the business.

We then move on to explore the importance of formalized meetings and give you a standard format that you can use as your own agenda for your business.

We believe that by following this approach you will dramatically improve the way in which you control your business, and it will lead to a greater understanding of your future opportunities.

preparing the business

You may be tempted to omit this chapter, or simply to pay it lip service on the basis that your business is a small business or a family-owned company, such that you do not have a formalized board of directors.

Understand the different relationships between shareholders, directors and managers.

If indeed there are sufficient number of directors in your business for you to perceive a board meeting to be worth while, you may often convene these meetings in a pub, coffee house or other informal locations.

However, there are immeasurable benefits to formalizing your board of directors in such a way that you are able to control your business rather than simply talk about it. Another advantage of formalizing your board is to make you and your fellow directors aware of your legal and fiduciary responsibilities, which is something most small businesses choose to ignore. Before we go on to examine a board of directors, it is absolutely essential to understand the different relationships that exist between shareholders, directors and managers.

Shareholders: A single or number of individuals, who own shares in a business in order to increase the value of those shares and to take an annual payment called a dividend. These shareholders only talk to the business at shareholders' meetings, at which point they will instruct their board of directors by simple majority vote on issues. The shareholders elect the main directors by voting at the annual general meeting.

Board of Directors: The managing director, who is appointed by the shareholders by majority vote, will appoint other directors or senior individuals as he sees fit, in order to run the business for profit. He will adhere to the memorandum and articles of association, which are the rules by which the shareholders wish the business to run. The board of directors (or, in smaller companies, a board of management) will meet periodically to discuss the performance, opportunities and strategy of the business.

It is a very important distinction, when you are running your business, not to be confused between shareholders and directors. Let us now dispel some of the myths.

KNOWLEDGE CHECKER

■ A shareholder can only instruct the business through formalized shareholders' meetings, which are called by the board of directors, unless it is a statutory annual meeting.

- It is important not to describe yourself as a director one day and the owner the following day. Your employment status is that of director in a limited company.

- A shareholder does not have to be a director.

- A limited company only needs one director and one company secretary.

- The company secretary is not a director, but is legally responsible for the housekeeping of the business, such as submitting Companies House returns. It is important to note that this role is very important because if returns are not made within the statutory timescales, your business will suffer fines and all of the directors of the board are legally responsible. The best book for further reading on a company secretary's role and duties is called the *Handbook of Company Secretarial Administration* by David Lintott, published by ICSA Publishing. For a more practical guide with illustrations there is another book available called *Be Your Own Company Secretary* by A.J. Scrine published by Kogan Page.

- The shareholders do not have right of access to the business or the right to receive any information without approval from the board of directors. Shareholders, who are not employed by the business, have no rights of control over any of the staff.

- The directors must behave in accordance with the Companies Act 1985/9 and, although this document is about 70cm thick, ignorance of its content or any of its clauses is not a defence in law. The best book that we have found for easy reading about all of your powers and duties are found in a Jordan publication called *The Company Director, Powers and Duties* written by Peter Loose, John Yelland and David Impey.

- Promotion to director status can be an euphoric event, but the legal responsibilities associated must be clearly understood before the Companies House Form 288a is signed by the individual.

- An appointed director will never be truly effective within the business and board unless he/she understands the powers and duties of the role in the first instance. Please refer the above point for further reading.

- It is absolutely essential that *all* directors undertake financial training, as you will find it is a very important part of the director's role.

It is not the purpose of this chapter to scrutinize the Companies Act, the role and duty of the company director nor that of the company secretary, as this is an area of further specialized reading or training.

preparing the business

The board meeting

> **Minutes to be discussed and approved by majority vote.**

The following is dedicated to the content of a board meeting. Please refer again to our earlier business model: the raft with the board of directors described as its rudder.

You will now notice that the training courses have followed the analogy of the raft in terms of the financials (keel), sales forecasting (sails and mast) and the organizational theory of a business (raft base).

CHECKLIST FOR THE AGENDA

- Date and venue of proposed meeting
- Invited list
- Agenda item 1 – to formally approve the minutes of the previous board meeting
- Agenda item 2 – to discuss the matters arising from this previous meeting
- Agenda item 3 – the business overview
- Agenda item 4 – the sales report
- Agenda item 5 – the financial report
- Agenda item 6 – any other business
- Agenda Item 7 – date of the next meeting

CHECKLIST FOR THE MINUTES OF A BOARD MEETING

- Company name and venue of board meeting
- Date and time of the meeting
- List of those present with job titles
- Minutes to be discussed and approved by majority vote with all amendments noted by hand. This copy should be signed by the chairman and company secretary and committed to file. It is recommended that there should only be one copy of the minutes and they should be signed and put in a fire-resistant cabinet. Therefore, any copies of draft minutes circulated to other directors should be passed back to the company secretary for shredding.
- *Matters arising.* In the previous board meeting these matters will have been assigned to individuals. Their reports should now be taken against each action and the outcome minuted.

- *The business overview*. This is normally delivered by the managing director or senior partner. It is an overview of the business activity for the previous month, which sets the scene for the board meeting, explains its focuses and leads on to the other detailed reports.

- *The sales report*. This attached written report must detail the agreed measurements of the business such as sales turnover, gross margin, size of order book, expected sales level for the next month, and any issues or difficulties experienced in the marketplace.

- *Financial report*. This attached written report deals with the detailed accounts of the business for the previous month and should give rise to a profit and loss account as well as a balance sheet and cash-flow indicator. This report often refers to budget variances as well as the bank account levels and expected debtor and creditor timings.

- *Other specific issues*. These must be agenda-d in advance otherwise they will be handled under any other business. These will be relevant to your business, but the important thing to remember is to make them strategic and not operational.

- *Any other business*. Anything that has arisen of a minor nature that has not been agenda-d in advance.

- *Date of next meeting*. The date of the next meeting should be confirmed with all directors.

- The meeting must be declared closed and agreed by majority vote.

preparing the business

SAMPLE OF BOARD MINUTES

MINUTES OF A MEETING OF [COMPANY LIMITED]

Date: 21 April 1998
Time: 9.30 am
Venue: ABC House, Town
Present: P Wells
                B Weston
                M Wilton
                J T Risto

ACTION

1   Minutes of the meeting of 12 March 1998

The minutes were tabled and 'once discussed' were approved.

2   Matters arising

2.1 JTR confirmed that a new bank mandate for MW as a cheque
signatory had been requested.

2.2 JTR had obtained details of the rent chargeable for the ninth floor
from Peter West. On the basis of the information received, the cost
of the office was approximately £880 per annum. It was agreed
that an inclusive charge for rates, service charge and rent of £1000
would be charged by the Sister Company to [Company Limited].
JTR agreed to pass these details onto Peter West

2.3 PW confirmed that he had given a presentation to Partners on 30
March 1998. It was agreed that this would be extended into other
departments and initially start with a presentation to the audit
department.

2.4 PW confirmed that a new cheque book had been received.

2.5 It was noted that Dave Bolton from the audit department had
helped with the preparation of the Sage accounts. It was agreed
that the small audit department would help on an on-going basis
which JTR would co-ordinate.

2.6 PW confirmed that he would be following up RIT's London contacts
separately. It was also noted that RIT would be suggesting one
good customer for the company to follow up.

2.7 It was noted that the Website for Sister Company was not ideal and
when PW had some time he would follow this up.

2.8 PW agreed to follow up with DR which mailshot had been sent out
in respect of Year 2000. It was noted that the Liverpool address
should be included on the mailshot, and DR would confirm which
clients had been targeted.

2.9 PW confirmed that he was following up other potential contacts
including venture capitalists.

ACTION

2.10 PW confirmed that he has met with London's consultant, Jim Dilt. PW is to hold further meetings with JD and possibly meet other contacts in the London office. At present, London are looking at bringing in a product similar to Prove It 2000 and there may be some common marketing areas. PW confirmed that it would be a useful strategic alliance, which could be developed. PW would provide the board with continual updates on this relationship.

2.11 JTR confirmed that he had met up with Perfect Computer Services and was waiting for them to come back with any follow-up to the services that could be provided.

2.12 PW confirmed that he would follow up the appropriateness of an insertion in the firm's brochure. He would also be providing continual notice board information to let staff within the firm know what was happening in the consulting division. It was noted that a three-page brochure is being produced which would be presented to the board for approval.

3 Chief executive's report

3.1 It was agreed that BW speak to Stephen Clagg regarding the opportunities in the Birmingham office.

3.2 PW agreed to set up a seminar/advertising strategy for the Midlands and invite Stephen Clagg to come along to that.

3.3 It was agreed that when appropriate JTR would review the controls and procedures in place for payment of creditors and approval of invoices, etc.

3.4 Although PW is disappointed with the performance to date, he feels that there are strategies in place which will move the business forward.

3.5 It was noted that there was a good variety of experiences that associates are bringing to the table.

4 Financial report

4.1 It was noted that PW's intention was to reforecast the budgets on an Excel spreadsheet and then monitor the performance against budget.

5 Marketing issues

5.1 It was noted that seminars are planned to run in April and May.

5.2 It was noted that PW would be holding a monthly marketing meeting with DR to focus on the company's marketing strategy.

5.3 It was noted that the company would be refocusing its seminars alongside those of the growing business seminars.

preparing the business

5.4   PE is to try to obtain a copy of John Dilt's marketing strategy. It was noted that MW's department is also refocusing its strategy and this would be cross-communicated to the company to take advantage of any synergy.

5.5   It was agreed that the company needed to concentrate on its profile over the next three months and target clients who will give a stream of work.

5.6   It was noted that the internal marketing and communication is the key to the development of the business.

5.7   It was noted that XYZ was potentially an attractive business to run alongside the profile business of the consultancy arm. It was agreed that the company needs to have a patient approach and despite the frustrations ensure that we concentrate on obtaining quality work.

6   Accounts and administration

6.1   It was noted that the accounts system was now in place and the company was able to track and monitor the payments of creditors. It was noted that the invoicing was not yet being produced from Sage.

6.2   It was noted that Dorothy Net has been taken on in administration. This position would be monitored and PW is hopeful it will turn into a full-time position if the business can justify it.

7   Any other business

7.1   It was agreed that we need to monitor the purchasing arrangements for the company which currently is being done via Sister Company. There appears to be some difficulties in administering the items purchased by Sister Company in Town and some things seem to be very expensive. This position will be reviewed.

8   There being no other business, the meeting closed.

Etiquette and style of a board meeting

Holding a board meeting is very much like having a dinner party. You can make it as formal as you wish, and the etiquette and style is entirely up to you.

There may be some of you who would like to know how to formalize a board meeting, and to help you to do this we have prepared a few tips and word styling which you can adopt for your own board meetings.

We felt rather uncomfortable in the early days when our company just consisted of seven employees and we were holding formalized board meetings. We quickly overcame this feeling when we came to realize that the board meeting was an important occasion and was an opportunity for us to develop ourselves and our business in a way which our daily operations meetings would never do.

TIPS AND PHRASES

- The appointed chairman may say, 'I bring this meeting to order and convene (time).' The memorandum and articles of association will describe the number of directors that need to be present at this board meeting in order to form a quorum.

- A vote can be formally requested by any agenda' item or issue of importance that arises from discussion, which becomes an important action for the board to adopt. This can be done using the phrases 'I hereby move that ...' and 'Can I please have this motion seconded'. Upon receipt of a seconded vote, the chairman requests that hands be raised in a 'for and against' count, and the words used are 'All in favour, please raise hands'.

- The minutes should record that a vote is either carried unanimously or carried with a majority. If a dissenting individual director wishes to reinforce his personal view, the minutes should recall this at his request. His words would normally be to the board, 'Please let the minutes record ...'.

- The minute-taker should use people's initials rather than full names.

- The minutes must record sufficient detail such that all important statements, arguments and comments are recorded accurately. This does not mean that every word and sentence should be written down, but summarized in short and concise sentences.

- The appointed chairman has a role to control the meeting to the agreed agenda and chair the interplay of discussions. In a small business you will find this is impossible, and so the chairman must be able to switch between the chair function and the director function several times during a discussion.

■ Board meetings should be held monthly and take place during the working day rather than out of hours which often reduces the effect of a board meeting. Meetings should last no longer than 2 to 4 hours.

■ There is sometimes a need to adjourn a meeting halfway through if, for example, a quorum of directors is not present in the room or the chair wishes simply to stop the meeting for a specific task or for a comfort break. This is normally phrased, 'This meeting is hereby adjourned at (time)', and this must be recorded in the minutes. To restart the meeting, 'This meeting is reconvened at (time)'.

■ To close the meeting, the standard wording is 'If there is no other business, I hereby move that this meeting be closed. Can I please have a seconder?'. A majority vote will close the meeting.

■ Board meetings should be held off-site where possible, but if they are held in your normal office environment, you should ensure that this time is free from interruptions, either by telephone or by staff.

Summary of chapter

We invite you to discover the answers to the following questions as the final part of your management training. This was, in fact, the management training modules that we used to train our own management team which likewise can be used to train your own team.

This is split into 6 weeks' work, which should be performed in addition to your [manager's] normal job duties. Some of the questions do not have definitive answers, but are meant to stimulate thought and discussion. If you [your manager] does not know the answer to any question, your role as a manager, in fact, is to discover the answer using resources available.

Week 1: Companies' legal structure

■ Why do companies exist?

■ Name the four most common companies.

■ What are the advantages and disadvantages of limited liability status?

■ What is a share?

■ Do you have to own shares to be a director?

■ When are the directors personally responsible for the company?

- What are articles of association?
- What is the Company Act and on what date was it passed?
- What is the minimum number of directors to make a company?
- Do companies have to pay tax? If so, at what rate?
- What significance does the date 6 April have?
- Why do we produce year-end accounts?
- Explain what we mean by 'net before tax'.
- What are the two stages of work that the accountants perform on limited company accounts at year-end?
- What is the turnover threshold for small limited company audit?

Week 2: Finance and accounting

- What is a nominal code and why do we use them?
- Explain a creditor and a debtor.
- List the points of information contained within a balance sheet.
- What does the profit and loss account tell us?
- Why are these often produced monthly?
- Why would your suppliers wish to see them?
- Who are Dunn and Bradstreet and who uses them?
- Name two institutions you can approach to request other companies' accounts.
- What is an acid test?
- What is a quick ratio?
- If you have a board meeting and the acid test or quick ratio is less than 1, what should the directors do?
- On what criteria would you select your accountants?
- List the functions of a company solicitor.

Week 3: Sales and marketing

- What factors in your opinion make up the image in your company?
- Describe your Unique Selling Point.
- What do we mean by 'demand creation'?
- List the six key stages a salesman must go through to achieve a sale.
- Which stage is considered to be the most important?
- List what you consider to be a good salesman's personal qualities.

- Why should salesmen have targets?
- How should these targets be calculated?
- What happens if they are not met with respect to the salesman and with respect to the company?
- Why is a salesman paid commission?
- Why is it important to measure a salesman's outgoing telephone calls?
- What else can we measure about a salesmen?
- How often should we do this?
- Is it good to promote competition by publishing these measurements?
- How important is the office support to the success of the salesman?
- Design a short 'cold call script' as if you were a salesman selling your company's product or services.

Week 4: Operations

- List the job types of people who would be employed in operations.
- If operations support sales, why doesn't the operations manager report to the sales director?
- Does the capabilities of an operation department ever affect your company image?
- Is the business development function ever part of operations?
- What does the business development function do?
- Is finance ever part of operations?
- What does the company secretary do?
- Using a recent historic profit and loss account of your company, calculate the percentage overheads to the turnover.
- Is this the average breaking point?
- What was this particular month's breakeven figure as a percentage of turnover?
- Using six consecutive profit and loss statements, plot your company's breakeven point by month as a percentage on a graph.
- Find the accounts for two of your competitors and decide if your overheads and net profits are comparable to theirs in percentage terms.

Week 5: Law and accounting

- List the stages of debt recovery which your solicitor would use.
- Describe a small claims action.

- What are the chances of success of recovery if a debtor refuses to pay a £1600 bill?
- How long will it take to follow this process?
- What happens if the court summons has your name or address incorrectly detailed?
- What does 'set aside' mean?
- Why are terms and conditions so important?
- Why do we insist on English law?
- What are the costs of pursuing a debt in court?
- List the factors whereby management will decide not to pursue a debt.
- What happens if you don't pay your revenue bill?
- What happens if you don't pay your VAT bill?
- What is the difference between cash-flow and net profit?
- Where is the cash in your business?
- Can you access it quickly?
- What is factoring?
- What is a debenture?
- What are director's guarantees?
- Are any of the above three ways of releasing or making available cash for the running of your business?
- Which one would you choose and why?

Week 6: Planning

Project

Consider all of your departments' direct budgetary costs. Examine the historical spend level.

Plan out the anticipated costs, by month, for the next 12 months of trading:

- assuming no growth in revenue or additional people
- assuming growth of 10 per cent revenue and 10 per cent additional staff.

Present this report as (1) base business, and (2) plus development business, clearly defined.

The answers to all of the above management training questions can be found on the diskette [■ **Management Training.doc**]

preparing the business

It is very important for your personal development that you work through these management training weeks for yourself, rather than be tempted to make a beeline to the answer file. At the end of this session you should be extremely well equipped in starting/running and developing your own business.

> We have found that the extension to your business knowledge through **continual training will keep you running your business successfully.** The ability to do this is tough when you have a busy schedule, but try to find time. In doing so, it will stretch your knowledge and abilities, therefore offering you a greater ability to solve or anticipate problems.

Now that we have completed the 'Training to stay alive' chapter, we have completed the 'Preparing the business' section, and are ready to move on and focus on the next part: 'Controlling the business' . This covers the most cited reasons for stress for most entrepreneurs: sales, and the management of people to make sales happen.

PRACTICAL STEPS

- Understand your business by getting to grips with all the accounting terms.

- Understand your operating statement and balance sheet in order to leverage your assets.

- Identify your base business and then plan to develop your business in a controlled fashion.

- Qualify your sales prospects by following the 10-point guide.

- Never be tempted to relieve yourself from the responsibility of
  – sales performance and customer relationships
  – the daily cash position of the business.

- Structure your business correctly by referring to the organisational design rules.

- Develop your skills in line with the phases of development required from the position of Managing Director.

- Complete the function analysis chart to understand whose function is critical to the positive cash-flow of the business.

- Complete the management training modules and then ask your management team to complete it as part of their personal development programme.

preparing the business

controlling the business

sales and marketing strategies

Sales

Marketing

Customer retention

The purpose of this chapter is to raise your awareness of the opportunities available to your business in either (a) leveraging sales through route to market or selling techniques, or (b) through marketing techniques.

We will dedicate time to looking at the various ways of using:

- modern-day marketing to increase your sales
- models of selling
- ways of measuring sales and the sales staff within your business
- ideas as to how to overcome low sales*
- measurements that you must take in order to analyze your sales to improve your business performance.

* This area will be explored in Chapter 8 in more detail, but will be covered in this chapter in the context of sales and marketing strategies only.

Don't wait for your ship to come in, row out to meet it.

Let's consider the act of marketing for a moment. We are now going to ask you to take a piece of paper and to write down in just 20 seconds the name and the model of just four small cars that you see advertised every night on the television. Now write down four brands of chocolate that you like the best. Notice, we said 'brand' and not 'name'.

You may be quite surprised that in the space of the 20 seconds you may not even be able to list four names of cars or four brands of chocolate. What does this prove?

Well, all of the brands that you listed have been sitting dormant as a message in your brain as a result of a TV marketing campaign launched by the manufacturer. This message however doesn't actually _sell_ to you, the dealer or shop does that. If it stocks the brand you like, you will buy it, or if not, you may go elsewhere or be tempted to switch to your second choice.

The same premise applies in business, whether you sell direct to the consumer, or sell your product or service to other businesses. Whatever you do in your business, at some point you will have to reach out to the customer in such a way that he/she will purchase something from you, which you will provide for profit.

There are many different ways of selling, and even more ways of marketing your products and services, and this chapter is given over to exploring just some of them. If selling is not one of your key strengths, consider a formal training course, as this is one aspect of your business that will never go away.

Remember – nothing happens in your business until a sale is made.

Whatever you believe your business does, and however stable or profitable your company has become, there is *nothing* more important than sales and this activity must command regular and undiluted attention from you as a business owner.

It is often tempting to hire a sales manager or even a sales director at this stage, who will come along to fix all of your sales problems. Whilst this can strengthen your sales ability as a company, use the information contained later in this chapter to measure and assess the effectiveness of your sales manager and sales force, and step in early if things are not going according to plan.

> **There is *nothing* more important than sales**

In our own business, there were three occasions when we thought that we could 'hand over' sales to our sales managers or even sales director. Things went well for a while, until we hit a quiet patch, and our own entrepreneurial skills were the only thing that could pull sales though. Our business lost over £100 000 in 3 months, as our sales manager struggled to use textbook sales techniques to put things right. When he resigned, we took the business back to basics, removing all of the systems and procedures that had become barriers to gaining sales. (Even though these techniques were technically correct for our size of business, the reason for the growth stemmed back to our opportunistic style.) It is quite incredible how far removed from your ideas your business can become if you truly delegate something like sales for even a year. Nine months after this catastrophic quarter, we had turned the £100 000 loss into a total profit for the year of £70 000.

Our advice is simple ... never, never, never, take your eye off the sales ball.

We are now going to consider the art of selling, and then later in this chapter move on to consider the various marketing approaches that you can employ in pursuit of the sale.

SALES

What is 'sales?' Well, simply put, it is the art of forming a relationship with a potential or existing customer. It is important to understand the relationship within the context of your marketplace and to take the appropriate measurements to improve sales.

How do we measure sales?

The sales of your company can be measured in many ways. You may be forgiven for thinking that there are only one or two, because that is the traditional style of sales measurement. In the modern-day approach, we are going to use information technology simply to gather information about sales, and then use this information to dramatically increase our sales.

Let's think of the various measurements that we can focus upon as sales managers of our business.

Turnover

This is the measurement of the total value of the sales (not including VAT). This is measured in pound notes and is sometimes referred to as the poundage in marketing terms. This is also referred to as the gross sales or 'top line'.

Gross margin

This is the total sales less the associated materials purchases that are required to complete the job. This is expressed either in pounds or in percentage of gross sales. Therefore a £1000 gross sale with a £400 materials purchase would generate a gross margin of £600. The gross margin percentage is therefore 600/1000, which is 60 per cent. Typically, this margin would apply to a manufacturing or a consultancy-type operation. If your business is in the services or reselling markets, as many are, your gross margin may be much lower. In our own computer services company, we managed our new sales on just 18 per cent gross margin, our used computer sales returned a better 30 per cent margin, and our virtual reality modelling business returned a wonderful 90 per cent margin. By having these figures to hand, it becomes clear to you, as directors, managing partners or owners, the opportunities in the various market sectors.

Gross profit

The sale minus the direct costs. This is different to the gross margin, as it takes into account the direct costs of providing the sale. For instance, if the sale illustrated above meant that direct factory staff laboured with a measured cost of £150 per item, the gross profit would be shown as: sale of £1000 less the materials cost of £400, leads to a gross margin of £600. Take away the direct costs of £150, and the gross profit will be £450. The gross profit margin will then be 450/1000, which is 45 per cent. By measuring this aspect of the sale we can start to assess the efficiency of our direct labour force, and make the 'make or buy' decisions that will increase our profitability.

It is the objective of the sales effort of any business to generate sufficient gross profit, such that, after deducting the known overheads of the business, there is something left over. We know this as net profit before tax.

For the purpose of the chapter, we will concentrate on the generation of sales and margin, which will allow the business to exist in the first place.

Models of sales

Depending upon which market and product you are associated with, you will be faced with a choice of how to sell to your customers. This is often called 'route to market'. For example, in our business we ran a direct sales force and a telesales force. They both existed for a reason, but gave quite different results. We would now like to examine the plus and minus points of each type of sales operation, but remember, just because it is the *norm* to sell in a certain way, it doesn't mean to say it is the best or the most efficient way of reaching the customer.

■ Direct salesforce

This mean that you and/or your salesforce will be making direct calls and visits to customers, presenting the product or service, and closing business.

Pluses
- Greater control over the sales message
- Can be the only way to sell a high value product
- The customer can feel better cared for

controlling the business

- Other opportunities can be found once the salesman is on site
- Buying 'clues' can be seen in customers' offices.
- Long-term or high-value relationships can be better forged

Minuses
- Direct sales staff almost always require higher basic salaries
- Company cars often form part of the package
- Other perks like pensions and health insurance are normal in some industries
- Mobile telephones and portable PCs, expense accounts need to be considered
- Direct sales staff need careful monitoring as they often use company time for non-company activity
- Lead generation is not something that a direct salesman does very well
- Unless these sales staff are in front of customers for the majority of time, they make for expensive telesales or sales support people.

This type of sales is very often the first one that a business owner will use when he/she sets up the business. It is vital for the continued development of the company that the board regularly considers other sales models in pursuit of greater profits.

■ Indirect salesforce

These are often the people that you may call internal sales people. They can be a cross between tele-selling and sales support, and can hold the customer relationship just as closely as the direct sales people. They hardly ever visit customers and make extensive use of the telephone and facsimile machines. More recently, the use of the Internet e-mail has been added to the sales armoury of the indirect salesperson.

Pluses
- Basic salaries are very much lower than the direct salesperson
- There are no additional costs in terms of cars, expense accounts, mobile telephones
- Management is easy, as they are office-based for most of the time.
- Span of management control can be increased from, say, five direct, to, say, nine indirect sales staff
- The company retains better control of the customer, as one internal sales person can easily be replaced by another
- Hiring costs can be lower due to the lower salary.

Minuses

- There can be less customer control if physical meetings never take place
- The internal sales position can be a short-term one from the employee's perspective
- The buying signals can only be read by telephone
- If your competitor wheels in a direct sales person, you are likely to lose control of the customer.

> **There can be less customer control if physical meetings never take place.**

■ Telesales

This is similar to the indirect sales person, but is, in fact, different. The teleseller is focused upon pure sales or lead generation. Such a person does not usually hold the customer relationship, and very often this activity is outsourced to an agency. This is done by providing a sales script and a target customer database. The agency staff simply work their way down a list, trying either to gain commitment for the product, or simply to make appointments for the direct salesman.

The interesting point about outsourcing telesales work is that there are various ways of paying for this service. In our company, we used telesales agencies for making appointments for our direct sales force, who were paid handsomely to be in front of customers and not managing their diaries to suit themselves. We paid the agency only for the confirmed appointments, which equated to approximately £40 per appointment.

Pluses

- Costs can be matched to output with no regular overheads
- If using an agency, the service can be turned on and off to the business need
- There are no additional overheads whatsoever
- Can also be used to clean databases by checking the details ready for a mailshot.

Minuses

- Can be too far removed from the customer
- In certain markets, the customer may be swamped by 'me too' telesales companies
- The sales message or the agenda for the meeting may be lost if not properly scripted

controlling the business

■ You are nearly always responsible for the script writing, which may not be your strength.

■ **Agency sales or commission-only salesmen**

Used in certain markets to increase coverage without increasing costs. These individuals work for a percentage of the sales they make, and rarely have a retainer fee or, in some cases, even their expenses covered.

Pluses
■ There can be no overhead at all unless a sale is made
■ Incremental business is easier to gain
■ The commission-only sales person is totally focused upon selling and results.

Minuses
■ There can be a conflict between a totally focused sales person and customer care
■ There is difficulty in establishing quality controls, reporting and accountability
■ There is often lack of commitment as the sales person sells for the highest return to him/herself.

*In the marketing section below, we will also tell you how to increase your sales coverage massively by setting up **partnership selling activities**, which work tremendously well, once established.*

Sales training

There is often the need to train sales staff for many reasons. It may be that you have promoted an individual to a direct selling position, and wish to offer formal training. The circumstances of the customer base may have changed, and the method of approach may need a refresher course. There are many books given over to sales training, which are bought according to the individuals' specific needs. One of the most effective trainers that we have found, and which we have used in our business, is the Sales and Management Training (SMT in Poole, Dorset) run by Joe Windsor. His approach is both refreshing and informative, and is to be recommended. Our firm recommendation to you, as the business owner, is to take time to undergo formal sales training *yourself*. This will probably be one of the most informative courses that you will ever attend.

> Take time to undergo formal sales training.

Remember that your business revolves around sales, and that nothing happens until a sale is made. Ask yourself the question:

- *'If I were 20% more effective at selling, what would be the effect upon the sales line, or the turnover of the business?'*

Better than that, if you can learn how to sell without dropping the price all the time, how much more money could you make?

- *If you were able to make the same sales, but increase your gross margin by just 5 per cent, how much profit would you make?*

Remember that both of these increases will fall to the bottom line, i.e. generate more net profit, as the activity of the sale will be no more expensive than before. You have just become a tiny bit cuter and will reap the rewards accordingly.

We spoke at the beginning of this section about the measurements of the sales force, and we will now give you some more ideas about the aspects of your business.

TIPS FOR THE MEASUREMENT OF SALES AND SALES STAFF

Log each sale individually, and classify the following information
- turnover
- gross margin
- type of customer by market sector, i.e. retail, banking, manufacturing, etc.
- order frequency of the customer
- type of product and whether this is a planned or distress purchase.

By salesman, analyze the following
- total turnover in the month
- total gross margin in the month
- number of deals in the month
- type of product sold to which sector customers
- whether the targets have been met for the month (see below for target setting)
- the anticipated orders for the coming month
- the sales by location and the time of the month
- expenses per salesman per month
- the rate of sales closed versus the number of meetings attended. This should be expressed as a percentage and called the 'close rate' of the salesperson.

controlling the business

Measure the sales manager in a company-wide approach. He/ she is responsible for the performance of the team. You pay them to make the team perform to the agreed sales levels. If this is not happening, make sure that this fact is reinforced and that you don't end up accepting that an individual salesman's performance is the sole reason for the company failure. In our experience, it is easy to accept sales line failure, and the myriad of excuses that form the explanation, but far more difficult to spell out the fact that the sales manager is responsible for the make-up of the sales team as well as its performance. It is their job to ensure that the team is performing, or take the decision to replace members.

> **Measure the sales manager in a company-wide approach.**

Never mind the blarney! Sales are vital for your company's health.

Use the following checklist to develop your sales opportunities. Take time to question yourself or your sales staff carefully.

---

1 Do you know for sure that you talking to the decision-maker?

2 Is there more than one decision-maker?

3 Have you identified the sponsors within the customer's business?

4 Does your customer have budget for spend already approved?

5 Were you part of this process or were you invited to tender against a list?

6 Do you know who your competition is?

7 Has the customer bought from you before?

8 Has your customer received a written quote from you?

9 What is the timescale for the decision?

10 Do you have free access to the directors of your customer?

11 Do you have a diarized close meeting set up yet?

12 Has the customer given you feedback from your proposal?

13 Are you more expensive than the competition?

14 Do you know on what criteria your customer will select suppliers?

15 Have you handled all of the customer's objections yet?

16 Have you fully explained the benefits to the customer's business as a result of buying from you?

In stating all the above, one of the hardest lessons that we learnt was that you, as the business owners or directors, will never relinquish responsibility for the *results*. If you try to do this too early in the development of your company, you could find that the sales manager has insufficient experience to carry out the task, as you would have done.

Indeed, we can recall one of our largest and most valued customers in London, during the time of rapid growth of our business. They were a large money broker in the City, but valued our dedicated service as a small business. It was the personal service and competent technical advice from us as the founders that was the unique selling proposition. As we grew, our time was taken up in controlling the growth and the financial aspects of the business. We decided that it was no longer a good use of our time to service this client directly, and so, in a one swift move, we appointed a sales person to the account. Business was so brisk that we didn't even have the time for a formal introduction, and so a telephone call became the method by which we handed over control.

Within 3 months we had lost all business from the account, and then lost control completely to our known competitor.

In a last-minute attempt to recover, we held a meeting with our valued customer, who was reluctant to tell us that he felt neglected, having moved from the owners and directors of the company looking after him, to a mere sales person. Sadly, we never recovered the customer, and lost a valuable piece of business. *An expensive and never-forgotten lesson that you can learn at no cost.*

Never disengage from your customers as you grow the business. Always maintain a handle, or at least hand over the *daily control* only, in a sensitive and professional manner.

There is unbelievable power in your personal contact with your customers. If they know they are dealing with the owner, they usually believe in the outcome far more than if your salesman

> People like to feel important.

says exactly the same thing. People like to feel important, and if the MD comes to see them, then that must surely boost their ego. Don't underestimate the power of your title, and never abdicate responsibility for the customer to your sales team.

Making every employee a salesperson

It seems so obvious, but every time your staff speaks or writes to a customer, there is an opportunity to gain information, deliver information, impress your customer or, failing all of those, miss the point entirely.

controlling the business

You can all remember doing this yourself. You call a business or a retail outlet, the phone might be answered promptly. The person to whom you speak is cheerful, informative, and asks you questions that you don't mind answering. The experience of talking to a professional, happy person is sufficient for you to open up a conversation and you leave the call having had a good experience with the company, which reinforces your original decision to deal with them.

Alternatively, you may make the same call. The telephone rings forever, finally to be answered by a person who is obviously not interested in your needs. Indeed, they seem anxious to get you off the phone, and you leave this call having had a poor experience, and neither party will be any the richer for it.

The first one, we hear you cry, that's got to be us! But is it? Have you trained and tested your staff for this outcome, and have you put in place the reward scheme of sales lead generation that will ensure that your staff will proactively follow this method of handling customers.

Remember that every employee is a sales person, no matter what his or her function.

In our business we put in place a retail voucher for £20 for each lead submitted by a non-sales staff member that led to a salesman closing a sale. This focused the business in providing a steady stream of information about companies in the area, and the possible sales opportunities arising.

> **Devising a commission scheme can be a difficult exercise.**

Our employees came to recognize the importance of sales, and the prospect of being responsible for a sale to the company, and the resulting public recognition became exciting for them.

In business we must leverage every possibility and leave no stone unturned in our pursuit of sales.

Commission schemes

We have found, in our experiences of talking to many businesses, that devising a commission scheme can be a difficult exercise. In this section we will discuss some of the ideas that will help you form your bespoke scheme. Don't be tempted to give this responsibility to the sales manager, as his motives are purely focused upon the measurement that you have set for him, and may not work for the business as a whole.

At one point in our business, we found that, in a particularly poor month, when we had not even covered the basic overheads of the business, and were therefore losing money, we were still paying some commission to sales staff who had not even made their target. This may be true in your own business, and perhaps a commission scheme change is just what you need to chase up the sales performance.

> Your business will be measured by turnover or by gross profit.

Here are some basic planning statements.

■ Understand that your business will be measured by turnover or by gross profit. If the sales staff have control of the gross profit margin, i.e. they can perform a cost plus calculation when quoting the customer, use the gross profit as the measure. If you sell by pricelist, and the margin control rests with the company alone, as is the case with some manufacturing and retail-based businesses, measure the turnover.

■ Sales targets must drive your business. Without these, you can never measure a poor performance, as there is no marker. Best efforts are not a sufficient yardstick for a performance discussion. What should your targets be set at? Well, the salesman's average in your business is a useful starting point, followed by an analysis of a similar business. By calling a competitor, and understanding how many sales staff they retain, then pulling a copy of their accounts, you can quickly divide the turnover by the number of sales staff to get an average.

■ Targets are highly emotive, as they represent the measurement and success or failure of an individual. Stepping the sales targets upwards regardless of other factors can demotivate your sales staff. Providing them with a little slack during the known quiet months can be a sensible move.

■ Before we move on to reward, perform the calculation of the overheads of the business divided by the number of sales staff. You will derive the bare minimum that a sales person will have to turn in each month in order for the company to break even (see breakeven analysis in 'Training to stay alive', Chapter 4).

■ This becomes the figure where you may chose to offer no commission whatsoever, as performance at or below this point will lead to a business loss.

■ The rewards after this point must reflect upon the breakeven point, but are not prescriptive. Just so long as you don't suddenly offer a healthy commission level over the breakeven point so that, after you have paid the commission cheque, your business falls into loss.

In our business, we implemented the following scheme, which we found successful.

Sales target set at £10 000 gross profit per month, as the salesman had full control of the margin by allowing him to quote the customer a cost-plus model.

- If the salesman earned just £5000 or below, he was paid no commission.
- If the salesman earned between £5001 and £10 000, he was paid only 5 per cent commission.
- If he hit target at £10 000, he was paid at a rate of 10 per cent for every pound he earned above the target.
- If he earned 120 per cent of target, his commission level rose to 15 per cent for every pound earned above this level.
- If he earned 150 per cent of target, his commission rose to 20 per cent for every pound earned above this level.

Sounds complicated? We would now like to analyze the above model, and see how the business and salesman view it.

■ The business view

In our business, we sought to prevent ourselves from paying commission when the business performed poorly. Our breakeven was determined at £4 500 per salesman. We therefore held the salesman to zero commission if the basic amount (with a small comfort zone for averaging) was not met.

For the salesman, we dangled a very small carrot for the under-target performance of £5001 to £10 000 gross profit. This served to keep him/her interested in making more sales in the same month.

Once target was met, the industry norm of 10 per cent was paid, but then we dangled a much better carrot. If the sales person overperformed in a single month, there was an escalator that meant he could earn substantially. The reason for this was clear. The business paid an overhead for the sales person in terms of car, basic salary, pension and health scheme contribution. If a target was met, and then exceeded, the additional gross profit earned mostly fell to the net profit line, as the overhead of the sales operation had already been paid for. The company felt that this overperformance could be rewarded with greater generosity, as shown in Table 5.1.

Table 5.1

Sold	Salesman earns (commission)	Company retains	Result for company
£2 500	Zero	£2 500	Discipline salesman
£6 000	£300	£5 700	Overheads covered
£10 000	£500	£9 500	Profitable by £5000
£12 000	£700	£11 300	Profitable by £6800
£15 000	£1 150	£13 850	Profit split
£20 000	£2 150	£17 850	Very profitable

Although the commission paid gets larger, the company is satisfied that the profits are solid, and is happy to share the profits with the salesman in order to incentivize him/her further.

> Overperformance commission was a real incentive to keep on selling.

■ The sales person's view

They understood that there was a threshold, which accounted for their basic costs to the business, and on most occasions they performed well above this level. The increment of 5 per cent motivates the closing of deals, even though the 10 per cent mark might not be reached due to a slow month.

This would reduce the temptation to *bag* the sale for the next month when they knew that they had orders coming in that would break the thresholds and earn them more commission. Nevertheless, this was still an option if they worked it out in advance. The sales manager tried their best to stop this happening, but the sales staff could force a bag if the commission scheme was weighted this way.

The overperformance commission was a real incentive to keep on selling even when the sales target had been met. If the higher levels were reached, sales people have an incredible ability to pull deals through early!

Table 5.2

Sold	Salesman earns (commission)	Company retains	Result for salesperson
£2 500	Zero	£2 500	Look for a new job
£6 000	£300	£5 700	Survive on basic salary
£10 000	£500	£9 500	£500 is better than nought
£12 000	£700	£11 300	Expected commission
£15 000	£1 150	£13 850	Big increase for just £3k
£20 000	£2 150	£17 850	Almost doubles with £5k extra

controlling the business

The salesman can see his commission payment rising from an overall percentage of just 5 per cent at £6000, to 10.75 per cent overall if he /she over-achieves (see Table 5.2).

■ Summary of commission

Your company will have its own culture of sales rewards. We have simply shown you the way in which you can structure a commission scheme for the good of the company as well as motivate your sales force. If you sell many products, you can consider having a sales target for the different lines, and therefore you can effectively control and reward your sales force as the business directs and not just as the salesman's best efforts to achieve the highest pay packet.

Purchasing for profit

Before we move on to look at sales databases, it is worth pointing out the importance of the purchasing function of the business.

The hardest part of the business is the closing of the sale. Once this is done, your business must do everything in its power to protect the profitability of the deal. Clearly, the most influential part of the sales delivery is the sourcing of the product or service. It is easier to describe purchasing as a function, but if you deliver man hours as the product of your business, consider your time and that of your employees as tradable commodity. Think of the amount of money that you cost your business, and put the appropriate resource into the job in hand.

Suppose, for example, you spend an amount of time each month in the sourcing of the product or service that you go on to sell to your customers. Suppose also you were able to save just 5 per cent of the price, just by asking, as most people do, and that you sold ten of these per month at, say, £100 each.

Then you would make a saving of £50 per month. That becomes £600 per year. If you did not choose to do this exercise, your business would have to make a further six sales at 100 per cent profit just to achieve the same position.

So, you can see the power of purchasing. Negotiate hard, use payment terms and bulk ordering as negotiating factors, and don't be afraid to ask.

Understand your suppliers. They too have month-end sales, end-of-quarter accounting periods, times when they are experiencing downturns in sales, and you must capitalize on these. Plot your suppliers' key dates, and ensure you push just a little harder on price at the right time. We guarantee that this exercise alone will increase the profits of your business.

Sales databases

In this modern age of selling, there are two forms of knowledge that will add value to your business. These are tacit knowledge and explicit knowledge. The difference between these is best explained by the method in which they are stored.

Explicit knowledge may be stored in a written procedure, a manual, or as a process within a computer database. It may be reproduced and reused in a consistent and repeatable way.

Two forms of knowledge are 'tacit' and 'explicit'.

Tacit knowledge is defined as 'understanding, implied, existing without being stated'. It is simply the things that we know, sometimes cannot explain, but it is knowledge that is contained within us.

The importance of this distinction is shown when we deal with sales information. It is vital that the company is seen to 'own the customer relationship' and we therefore must set about creating a record system in order to hold information whereby we can satisfy ourselves that the company is in control. Indeed, it is essential to record as much information that is relevant to the customer as possible, for the more that we know, the better our relationship can become.

Record as much information relevant to the customer as possible.

There are many contact databases on the market, some good and some not. It is important to understand the purpose for which you will access this information before you make your selection. For example, a simple Microsoft Outlook database will allow you to hold contact data, and then to perform a mailshot or a mail merge function for the purpose of marketing.

If, however, you need a time-alarmed package that reminds you of overdue calls, and into which you can enter complicated text identifiers and records associated with the customer, then you may wish to look at 1st ACT or Maximiser as a product. If you are running a remote sales force, who only come

controlling the business

to the office, say, weekly, the docking and security of a product called Multitask will be of interest.

Look around the market, using IT magazines, and your IT suppliers. Make your selection carefully, and ensure that the package will export to Microsoft Excel, as this makes the process of change in the future so much easier as well as being an effective pivot to the Word application for mail-merges.

A word about security. The database of a company is often accessed by all staff. Limiting this, or the access level, to just the staff that need to know, using password control, is a good business practice. Making the unauthorized copying of the data records should be a sackable offence, and the removal of the data should be made as difficult as possible.

If you are keeping records of any kind, even if they are contained on a card index system and not a computer database, you *must* register under the Data Protection Act the fact that you have this data, and conform to the law in this respect.

We opened this section by talking of tacit as well as explicit knowledge, and this was done to highlight the fact that, no matter how much data you record about your customer, there is still an element that you will never capture unless you have a direct relationship with him. This statement is meant to underline our comments above about *never* relinquishing the customer relationship completely.

In our business, we made it our function as directors to accompany sales staff to new customers, and to attend our seminars, even as we became a £6.5 million turnover business. The lesson of that early loss of our London customer rang in our ears for some time. We also matched each external sales person with an internal sales person. In this way, the relationship and the tacit knowledge was shared and duplicated. If the external or internal sales person left the business, there was always a back-up to the customer, and we maintained continuity of relationship.

A database can record many pieces of information that we will speak about in the marketing section to follow, but the retention of the tacit knowledge of a customer will ensure continued success to the business.

Before we move on to look at marketing concepts, we would like to share with you the objectives that we would consider setting for the sales manager and the sales person in a business. This is not meant to be prescriptive, but will hopefully give you some ideas about how to control the sales force more efficiently. You will first of all see the objectives of the managing director, and the statements about customers and sales.

Each subset of objectives as they cascade down the business should all add up to the sum total of the business's overall objectives. (See Chapter 7 for detailed information on how to manage a business using goals and objective cultures.)

OBJECTIVES OF MANAGING DIRECTOR

1 Re-style the board process to take account of the low risk but expansive stance of the business moving forward by [*date*].
2 Manage the sales department to return profit to the business on a quarterly basis.
3 Lead the business in the quarterly planning function, involving operative staff wherever possible.

> Take the lead in developing large or strategically important clients.

4 Coach the board directors in the fundamentals of planning, finance and accounting, and board process at a strategic level to be delivered by [*date*].
5 Undertake development work as agreed by the board from time to time and keep it clearly minuted.
6 Ensure the business has sufficient working capital on a weekly basis.
7 Ensure sufficient resources in terms of cash, people and equipment to run the business.
8 Take weekly written reports from sales, operational and finance functions in respect of control criteria.
9 Take the lead in developing large or strategically important clients, either by direct involvement or by indirect coaching of the sales force and visits to customers at least four times per month.
10 Chair the weekly management meeting.
11 Review all subordinates to company standard on a quarterly basis.
12 Delegate all other tasks to the appropriate department in order that the company gains stability and a responsibility culture and review with the board on [*date*].

OBJECTIVES OF THE SALES MANAGER

1 Devise a customer database which has sufficient functionality to categorize, record information, initiate and control mailshots and integrate to any marketing activity as may be required. To be completed by month 2 of joining the business.

2 Compile a list of prospective customers, historic customers and current billing customers within 4 weeks of appointment.

3 Compile a written report to the managing director by each Friday 12 pm., indicating the value of the current billings for month 1,2 and 3 forwards, the value and the name of the likely sales wins, and the sensitivity to this forecast.

4 Resource the sales department with sufficient staff to ensure that the agreed sales targets are met, working within the agreed budgetary amounts on a monthly basis.

5 Train all new sales staff in the culture of [company], issue agreed objectives within one week of start date. Measure formally on a quarterly basis, whilst taking at least weekly sales review meetings in order to comply with 3, above.

6 Report any out-of-line situations to the managing director in respect of customer issue, or to the operations director in respect of fulfilment, within 24 hours of occurrence.

7 Form selling partnerships with other organizations in order to increase the order frequency. Indirect sales to account for 10 per cent by turnover within 4 months.

8 Integrate and co-operate with [company] customer care programme as may be initiated from time to time.

9 Work with the MD to agree seminar, speeches, exhibition events, and any other marketing-led activity.

10 Ensure that the sales budgets are met on a monthly basis.

11 Attend weekly management meetings.

12 Review all subordinates to company standard on a quarterly basis.

13 Ensure company terms and conditions of sale are agreed at every sale.

OBJECTIVES OF AN EXTERNAL SALESMAN

1 Plan out, make sales calls to customers, prospects, current billing and historic, in order to identify business for profit on a daily basis.

2 Make professional presentations to customers in order to explain the benefits of [company] services and input the progress to the [company] database.

3 Close and take orders from customers to supply the services provided by [company] working in conjunction with Operations department resource plan, ensuring the customer is informed of timescale abilities, etc.

4 Make sufficient sales calls on a daily basis to ensure that the monthly sales targets are met.

5 Provide written report to the operations department in order for the contract to be correctly resourced.

6 Take sufficient weekly training in the products of [*company*] in order to sell the whole range of services

7 Input all required data into the sales database in a timely and accurate fashion as directed.

8 Integrate the customer care programme into the sales process, ensuring the client views the relationship with [*company*] as long term. Provide feedback to the operations director on a monthly basis in writing, classifying by customer.

9 Demonstrate an active and sufficient pipeline of business on a monthly basis, with a written forecast for the next month sales wins, as well as written report of sales losses.

You can see how the managing director has certain profit- and customer-focused objectives, and how these have cascaded to the external salesman with greater detail and controls. Thus, as the objectives move away from the director, the detail and controls become less strategic and more operationally driven.

These are some objectives that you may like to adapt or copy in your own business.

> **The managing director has certain profit- and customer-focused objectives.**

Don't forget, if you run a very small business, even one where you are the only sales person as well as the sales manager and managing director, the objectives can still apply to you as you change hats during the working day.

What happens if the sales don't come in as planned?

Finally, we come to the most frequently asked selling question in business. What happens when all the euphoric planning, all the anticipation and the projections, grind to a halt, as the sales line is not met?

■ It is essential, first of all, that you take time to understand in detail the reasons why the sales department failed to achieve the projected level of business. If you are a very small business, you may well be the sales department, but it is even more important that you now stand back and truthfully analyze the problem. Don't allow yourself or others to be persuaded of mysterious market forces that have temporarily robbed you of the business, or of that elusive huge deal that has slipped for the second month running.

controlling the business

■ If you don't know the reasons, lift the phone and speak to your customers; ask them why it is that their normal level of business was not reached. Speak to your suppliers, and find out if this pattern is replicated across your industry. You must know if this is a long-term problem, particular to your business, loss of market share to a single or multiple competitors, etc., etc.

■ *Examine the trends and patterns*, find out why the sales forecast failed, and be honest as to whether it will fail again. If so, then consider your business model, and examine the effect upon cash-flow. The cash squeeze resulting from low sales usually affects a business about 8 weeks after the event. If sales dip and then recover the next month, maintain your guard against poor cash-flow in the following months.

> There is never a substitute for sheer hard work.

■ When you have finished analyzing as above, and you have taken corrective action if needed, then *turn your attention to pure sales*. Cancel leave and holidays, postpone non-essential meetings and projects, and focus your staff upon the task in hand.

■ *There is never a substitute for sheer hard work*, as sales can simply become a numbers game. It is clear that, if you normally make ten phone calls, get four enquiries, quote in one of these cases and then close one in three, that you will need to make 30 calls on average to make one sale. If your business makes 120 calls per day, you should make four sales, and so it goes on.

■ *Lead by example if the sales are low*. Sit amongst your sales staff and get your hands dirty. People love to be led, and we personally never disappointed them in these situations.

■ *Adversity can often lead to a stronger team*, so make sure that you capitalize on these events, even though you may see them as one-off negative periods.

■ *Call existing customers first*. These people know you, and have bought from you in the past. It is easier to sell to a warm customer than it is to a cold call prospect who doesn't know you. You will probably find that, once you get to this stage, that some of your oldest customers have not been contacted for some time. You may also find that your sales staff may have forgotten a few of the basics about selling and, yes, if that salesperson is yourself, then you must recognize that this may be the case.

■ Use call windows to maximize sales time. The best time to call customers can vary between industry, but in our business, our call windows were:

08.00   Administration and planning by getting phone numbers ready, sales literature and call pads. The aim was that, once we got on the telephone, nothing would stop us until we chose to stop.

9.30   Sales time! The telephone was glued to the ear, calls were made continuously, and all incoming calls were queued unless they were a customer.

12.00   Stop calling, and start to write up the quotes. Take a quick break and then plan for the afternoon. Now is the time to call other traders and suppliers.

14.00   Start the sales call routine again, as per the above plan. It is easy to start to cherry-pick the 'nice calls' once you start to tire. Resist this temptation and call sequentially.

16.00   Stop calling, and take time to assess the day's work. Plan out the following day, and use the time until close of business to motivate your staff. Overemphasize the positives and use large helpings of praise. Be positive in front of your staff, and they will respond positively to you. Fail to act this way, and your staff will nod at you and then promptly go home and dig out the jobs' application section of the newspaper.

This can be a very vexing time for you, and we have experienced this at first hand on more than one occasion. In fact, we always remember the £100 000 loss, that we managed to turn into a £70 000 profit by the end of the year. For about 4 months of that year we were trading insolvently under advice from professionals but, more importantly, we placed the business under the very watchful eye of our very strong board. In this way, we traded legally, and recovered from the worst low sales period of our business lives.

We recollect certain characteristics of that turnaround, and we have listed them for you in the hope that you may never need them, but in the knowledge that you most certainly will at some point.

CHECKLIST FOR ACTION

When the sales become low, run down the following 17-point checklist

1   Recognize that the sales have not come in. Don't confuse yourself with excuses.
2   Analyze the reasons as quickly as you can. Run through the ideas shown above.
3   Communicate with your staff without delay. The order administrators already know that things are not going well. Tell them the truth about the poor sales results. Anything less than the truth will be discovered, and motivation will be lost.
4   Draw up a written-down plan. This plan must state a goal and a definite sales

controlling the business

number, which is turned into a company target for everybody to aim for, not just the sales staff. This profit must relate to a breakeven or a net profit figure. This way you can involve everybody in the business, and save money as well as make it.

5 Tell all staff of their responsibility to delay expenditure. 'It is far easier to save a pound than to make one.'

6 Don't panic employees. Make the event a motivational one. Use words that bind the staff into a mission rather then scatter them in every direction.

7 Lead by example. Cancel all non-essential meetings, come into the office earlier than usual, and stay later in the evening. Make obvious sacrifices in order to show your employees that you are the leader of their team, and not just the boss.

8 Launch a sales campaign in line with the ideas shown above. Use the call windows and the call planning techniques. Train all staff again in the art of selling and the product range. Make the process enjoyable and deliver the training yourself.

9 Get your administrative staff to use their time wisely by sending out mailshots to existing and new customers. Don't forget to use the fax machine for increased efficiency.

10 If your business holds stock, start to turn it into cash as soon as possible. You must maintain turnover, even at a smaller net profit, so long as it is a profit. The stock in your company is dead cash. You must turn it into operating capital to ride out the cash-flow problems that will come down the line in 2 to 4 weeks' time.

> **The stock in your company is dead cash.**

11 Call your suppliers and ask them if they have any 'specials' today, or any ex-demo equipment that you can sell for them at short notice. Tell them it is part of a sales expansion in your business, and then use this information to feed into the sales calls and the mailshots.

12 Extend the product range to your customers. Ask them what else you could supply to them. We remember that we even sold a desk and chair with the computer workstation as a value add-on to the customer. This method will enlarge your turnover and provide valuable cash-flow. If you are successful, this extended product range could be a future market for you.

13 Send out positive messages to all of your suppliers and trade colleagues. Nobody likes to hear of bad times, and the last thing you need right now is a credit-line reduction from your suppliers or bank.

14 Make sure that you have accurate financial information. Pay attention to the balance sheet, and seek the help of your accountant if you need an opinion as to the solvency of the business. Remember, it is illegal to trade whilst insolvent unless you comply with strict conditions. You are personally liable for this

state of affairs, so seek advice from accountants as soon as you need to.

15 With the exception of the above, refrain from giving any information of a financial nature to any other source, unless you have a very good relationship with them. Lending institutions have a nasty habit of giving knee-jerk reactions to difficult times in small business.

16 Monitor the sales and the cash on a daily basis. Know your numbers and keep a keen eye on the net result.

17 Draw up a second plan, but do not discuss this one with anyone. This is the crisis plan, and will give you the ability to see where the emergency cuts need to be made. This plan often includes redundancies or dismissals, but can also include the sale of assets to return cash to the business, injection of equity cash from third parties or injection of cash from you personally. Also consider the cancellation of overtime, the reduction of your and staff salaries for a short period and the postponement of all non-essential expenditure. In these plans, most entrepreneurs cancel all marketing spend as well. Before you do this, read the following section on marketing, as there are many ways to skin the cat.

We hope your plans will not be needed, or at the least the points that you use will only be 1 to 16. However, when the chips are really down, we hope that we have given you some guidance as to the process of recovery that you can use, that will get you back on track as fast as possible.

MARKETING

First let's consider three interrelated facts about running a small business.

■ An entrepreneur is in business to survive at all costs
■ All companies have a tendency towards instability and ultimately failure
■ Success stems from the ability of a company to continually exploit change.

So we return to the picture in our minds of the raft that was used to depict a business in Chapter 4: 'Training to stay alive'.

We know that your business is small, and that the turnover probably won't even register in the industry's market share statistics, and that means that we have to constantly promote our businesses in the chosen marketplaces, if we are to survive, let alone grow.

controlling the business

Marketing, even the simple word, arouses feelings amongst entrepreneurs in the UK that are almost always negative. The imagery of the marketing professional with his glass of champagne after a quick round of golf, off to have lunch to discuss a new campaign, often overrides the true potential of marketing in a small business. We worked in London during the yuppie era of the mid-1980s, and can testify to the crowds of marketing staff who regularly drank champagne, ordered by the crate, and can sympathize with your impression, even if this is, or is not, your opinion.

> **Marketing arouses feelings amongst entrepreneurs.**

Time moves on, and the recession of the early 1990s brought about fundamental changes which, along with the rapid developments in computing, have revolutionized the marketing function within all businesses. The advent of the publishing and pagemaker software packages for a small sum of money on a PC platform, has led to many businesses being able to design and produce their own literature and adverts.

With information technology pushing out the boundaries of our imaginations, we will now describe the various methods of self-marketing that you as a small business can use to tremendous effect. The use of the Internet and the associated technologies are explored in greater detail in Chapter 12, but they have had burgeoning effects upon the competitiveness of small business in the global and home markets.

If you have not considered marketing as a separate function to that of sales in the past, let's first of all simplify the distinction, and then look at some of the more obvious ways that you can market your business, products and services.

Marketing is the art of attracting a potential customer to your business, whilst sales is the art of converting your words into money.

Customers can be attracted to your business in a number of ways, but before we look more closely at the different ways of achieving this, it is absolutely essential that you understand what you sell.

Well, that's obvious, we hear you say, and it won't take me long to list them either. Or will it ?

What will you list when we ask you that question? Let's try it. Use a piece of paper, and list the first five things that you sell.

1 _____

2 _____

3 _____

4 _____

5 _____

We hope that you haven't listed your products, because that is *not* what you sell. You must think of the customer, and ask yourself 'Why will that customer lift the phone, come into my shop/office?' The customer will not do this to buy a product; he/she will buy from you because you offer a *solution*.

A purchase can be described in many ways – an essential purchase like food, a luxury purchase like a three-piece suite, or a convenience purchase like a Chinese takeaway; a distress purchase like a new tyre for your car, Paracetamol for

> The customer will buy from you because you offer a *solution*

headaches or a sweet for a screaming child! Whatever you sell, there will be a category for its route to market, and you must understand where you stand. It is vital that you understand what it is about your product or service that is bought for its problem-solving qualities.

The takeaway mentioned above solves a hungry and time-pressured person's need for food, or it may be a Saturday night treat instead of going out. If we were to ask you what type of person you would send a leaflet to, telling them of your delicious food, you might reasonably tell us that the middle-ground professional market would be the source of the customer. The 'stay in on Saturday night' brigade would be the young family across all social divides, and the price of the food would further hone down the target market.

Sounds easy, but then let's look at a business such as a furniture shop. Traditionally, this would be a luxury purchase, and deferred until it was absolutely necessary to replace or purchase. The industry itself despaired in the last recession, and finally analyzed their market. They found that there was a lot of people in the market that really did want to buy new furniture, but that the

controlling the business

price was a problem. Actually, to stop at that conclusion would have seen you go out of business. The price was the objection, but only in so far as the payment terms. Ask a customer to buy with cash down, and they will hesitate. Tell them to pay nothing for a year, and then pay interest-free over 3 years, and they'll snap your hands off. Increase the price to finance the whole deal with the finance house, and away they go. Averages of 40 per cent increase in profits have been estimated in recent times amongst the more successful retailers.

The retailers solved the customers' problems for them. The furniture was a luxury purchase, and the problem was cash-flow. Remove the cash-flow, remove the objection, and the furniture sells well.

So, where was the marketing lesson in this example? Well, the price objection is a common one, and the art of removing it, or finding a cheaper way to sell in order to match pricing, is where the art of marketing comes along.

■ Unique selling proposition

For the business that first thought of this idea, this method of selling became a unique selling proposition. It made them different to every other furniture business and gave the customer the added incentive to shop at their store.

Think hard, and record what you believe *your* unique selling proposition is. Don't mention the words 'customer care', or a 'better service'. Differentiate yourself in a succinct way. If you only had two sentences to describe what you can do for a customer that no other business can do for them, this is the statement that we are looking for.

When you have decided what this proposition is, use it and leverage it in all of your documentation and sales calls. Tell the world, for this is the difference that will convince the customer that you are the supplier for him, and no other.

We now move to look at the various techniques that you can consider for your business.

■ Advertising

The most common association with marketing adverts needn't be expensive, and they can be co-funded with your suppliers, for example. The most important thing to remember is that you must test the wording in the advert and the headline of the advert in order to maximize the effect. One of the most thought-provoking marketeers in this subject is Jay Abraham, who can be contacted via Nightingale Conent. His material is very useful if you want to explore this subject in great detail.

■ Editorial

The wonderful thing about editorial is that it can be free! We have had hundreds of editorial comments published over the years, and some with great effect. Remember that it must be written for the reader, in a tone that entertains or informs, and it must be something the editor wants to print. Most newspapers sell copy on stories, so if you can make your submission controversial, then even better. If you are uncertain about writing for yourself, employ the services of a PR company. If you submit articles in this way, you do have the benefit of free press, but beware, the news reporters write for sensationalism and your words and meaning may not end up in the form that you wanted.

> **News reporters write for sensationalism.**

> *Tip: Meet the editor of the local paper, and enlist his understanding as to what you are trying to do if you can't afford to employ a public relations person.*

■ Mailshots

With computers in just about every business these days, the use of the mailmerge function is widespread. You can use this to create a marketing or sales letter, and then merge it to a computerized database of names and addresses. With your time taken up selling, this can be an effective way of attracting enquiries and can be a powerful force working for you in the background. In our business, we used to send out about 400 mailshots per week. Remember, don't try to sell, try to solicit the enquiry. The selling activity is best done directly in most cases, as the control and the up-sell opportunities are maximized.

Think laterally now, and use the mailshot principle in conjunction with the fax machine. We used to send upwards of 400 faxes every night, 5 days per week, and the cost was extraordinarily low. The fax can be targeted in the same way as the letter, and often the incoming fax finds its way straight to the intended recipient's desk, rather than being weeded out by the secretary. See Chapter 11: 'Effective use of technology' for more information as to how to use the fax in this way.

controlling the business

■ Seminars

Running a seminar needn't be an expensive exercise, particularly as we would always tell you to charge for attendance. Most businesses start out down the seminar route by offering free places, and always wonder why so few people turn up. The reason is quite simple. If you don't charge, there is no commitment from the customer. He/she perceives the information that you will give to be of reduced value because, if it was worth something, surely you'd charge for it. We have run the same seminar twice in the past, one free and one with a £15 registration fee. We had nearly four times as many people attend the paying seminar than the free one. Every attendee can run to £25 or so, and the experience becomes enjoyable for both attendee as well as organizer, as there is a commercial bond in place.

> A seminar is a way of demonstrating how good your business is.

Why run a seminar in the first place? Well, it is an ideal way of demonstrating just how good you and your business really is. If you are not a great speaker, ask your suppliers if they will help you. They see this type of exercise positively as they can see a tangible attendance and a considered sales opportunity. Pick a subject that is of interest to a user group, then approach your local chamber of commerce and Business Link for assistance in either the funding or the marketing to a defined customer base. This is an excellent way of finding new customers for your business.

FIVE TIPS TO RUNNING A SEMINAR

1 Mailshot to a clean database, ensuring all details are correct
2 Charge for the seminar
3 Don't expect a huge response
4 Use the Business Link in your area to help you to find attendees
5 Make the subject interesting, and even team up with other businesses to run a longer joint seminar. Use guest speakers from your suppliers if you can.

■ Exhibitions

Usually a more expensive option than running seminars, but can be of value none the less. The important thing about exhibitions is to understand the total costs and stick to your budget. If you have a unique service or product, then an exhibition can provide an ideal launch platform, and inviting the press can give you much free publicity. We launched a virtual reality city on the Internet (*www.virtual-Derby.com*) at an exhibition, and ended up on Central News Television. Our firm advice is to take formal sales training as to how to run an exhibition stand.

That's right, there are special techniques to running a stand, and to get it wrong will be to throw away your opportunity to make the exhibition pay dividends.

SIX TIPS TO RUNNING AN EXHIBITION STAND

1 Ensure that you have sufficient budget available, as what you think it will cost you will undoubtedly not be enough

2 Make your stand exciting, informative and inviting

3 Do train your staff to approach customers professionally

4 Don't ever say 'Can I help you'! and don't stand to attention at the front of the stand as if you are guarding against marauders

5 Make your stand a data collection point, as you are unlikely to sell on the day

6 Follow up your contacts promptly and use a telesales operation if your response is large.

7 Don't neglect your existing business while you are exhibiting.

■ Public relations exercises

In the daily running of your business, there may be chances for you to capitalize on normal events, such that you can gain publicity in your local area. The most obvious are the things like donating your old unwanted equipment to the local school or charity. Be creative in the way that you consider public relations. If you recruit from the New Deal or unemployed sector, publicise this in your local paper. Public relations needn't cost anything, but can deliver huge benefits to you and your business.

> Public relations needn't cost anything.

■ Partnerships

This is possibly the most powerful marketing technique that you can operate in a small business. Ask yourself the following:

131

What could happen to your business if you were able to hire an additional ten sales staff on a commission-only basis, who were professionally dedicated to selling your product alongside their own complementary product?

A multiplication of profits, that's what would happen, in every conceivable way.

Think about what you sell, and then think about your customer. Is there a similar, but different product that you know your customer buys with roughly the same frequency as your own product? In our computer industry, we realized that the sellers of telephone systems were such a partner. By asking a reputable dealer if they would like to market computers to their customers, they saw this as a way to increase their turnover and profits. We saw it as a way to get very warm leads with no sales costs whatsoever. Both parties were winners, and the workload was equitable. We used other partners, such as stationery providers, who wished to sell low-end PCs in their catalogues, again to their established customer base.

You, too, can find such a partner. Think with an open mind, and involve your staff and family in the search for a complementary partner. There has to be an element of trust in the first instance, and you must promise each other to terminate the agreement if an invoice doesn't get cut within, say, 45 days. If it doesn't work first time, don't be discouraged, but try again. It often takes two or three partnerships to make a commercially attractive one happen.

When it does spark, it becomes worthwhile. You can enjoy a steady stream of sales leads, through which you will probably reach a commission agreement with your partner business. For the same sales overhead, you can now generate far greater sales, and so your profits will increase exponentially.

■ Brand extension

If you have developed a name in an industry, either as a business or as a product line, you may decide to extend the name to cover other less associated products. This is a method known as endorsement. The power of endorsing a product can be dramatic. Look back at the name Zanussi, or Hotpoint or Hoover. In the 1980s they all extended their brand to cover such diverse products as electric drills, tool sets, car wash products, and work clothes.

The power of the brand name was extended to add credibility to other products. The price could then reflect a quality brand price, despite the fact that they were all manufactured in China.

Never underestimate the power of the brand, and how it can be used to legitimize a product. It may even be considered in reverse. What might happen to your business if a major brand were to endorse your product or service, and the leverage you could achieve if you were to get agreement on this basis?

> Never underestimate the power of the brand.

■ Business networks

These are normally associated with the local Chamber of Commerce in your area. For their members there are often networking functions, sometimes with guest speakers available to entertain or inform you.

Whatever the purpose, if an opportunity comes about to mix with a group of businesses, you must consider attending. If you do so, you must be clear about your motives for being there.

Take with you a pack of your business cards, and talk to as many people as you can. Collect their cards, and then use the event to write to them the next day, or call them in order to arrange a meeting. This use of a common event can be a useful way of getting meetings with people who would normally be less accessible.

■ The power of the referral

If we were to have a pound for every time we heard entrepreneurs say that the most marketing that they ever did was word of mouth, we could have retired years ago!

> Word of mouth is one of the most direct forms of marketing.

The word of mouth is one of the most direct and beneficial forms of marketing that you will experience in business. If you have been in business for a while, you will know how easy it is to be asked to speak to a customer who has got your name from another one of your satisfied customers.

So states the power of the referral. But how many of you in business actively go about asking for the referral from your satisfied customers? If you think that you'd rather not, as you have seen the double glazing salesman do this, you may be forgiven for not thinking a bit more laterally.

- *There are many ways of asking your customers if they know of anybody who perhaps have similar problems to the one that you have just solved for them.*

controlling the business

- *Would it be possible that these people might benefit from an introduction to you? If this is the case, perhaps you could use your colleague's name in the opening call, in order to make it easier for the introduced person to take the call in the first instance?*

So you see that by scripting the request in a more professional and soft-sell method, it is possible to ask for referrals from your existing customer base.

We believe that setting up a formalized referral scheme within your business is a valuable marketing tool that will always generate profits for your business. Remember that the referral can come from customers, supplier, partner businesses, family and friends and, of course, your own employees.

CUSTOMER RETENTION

It takes months to find a new customer; only seconds to lose one.

We all know the saying, and we all nod wisely, but how many of us actually take the time and trouble to measure the customer retention rate. We believe that only a small number of businesses take the time to perform this incredibly simple, yet important, task.

| Measure the customer retention rate. |

How many customers will you sell to today, or this month, and how many of those will still be live, buying customers in just one year? If we suggested 15 per cent only, would you be shocked?

If you have been in business a while, we recommend that you analyze the sales base today, and compare it to the earliest sales report or sales day book that you can find. We know that you will be shocked at the low retention. If you are fortunate enough to know the customer retention rate, it is likely that you have bothered to stay in touch with your customer base, and that your rate of retention could be high, but this is not normal in small businesses.

Consider this: how much does it cost you in real hard currency, to plan, contact, visit, quote, demonstrate, close and deliver to a *new* customer. Now think what it costs to take an order from an *existing* customer. We know that you will discover that the costs can be as much as ten times that of the existing customer, because that was the figure that we came out with when we analyzed our own computer business.

We wasted so much good money chasing new customers, when the answer to our sales expansion was right under our noses in the existing customer base. Yet in the space of 4 years, we had not retained 60 per cent of our original customer list.

> *There are only three ways of increasing sales turnover:*
>
> **1** *increase the order frequency*
> **2** *increase the order value*
> **3** *increase the number of customers.*

We would like you to think in terms of the existing customer for a moment, and look at the first two points. If you retain the customer, by looking after his needs, it is highly likely that your customer will buy more frequently from your business. Furthermore, if you have extended your product offering, as we talked about in the sections above, the average order value will increase as well.

So, what is the effect of these points?

If you take a customer who orders widgets from you twice a month, at £100 per sale, then you will make £200 per month, which is £2400 per year. You will probably have a salesperson assigned to this account, and a structure of order taking and administration. Let's say, for the sake of argument, that the proportional cost of this support was £2000 per year. Your net profit, therefore, is £400 per annum.

If you managed to increase the order frequency by just three drops per year, and you were to increase the order value by just £5 per drop, what will be the outcome?

Total drops per year is now 27 (increased from 24), order value is now £105 per drop (up from £100). The turnover will have risen to £2835 (from £2400), which is an increase of £435. If we told you that your overheads to service the customer would only increase by 5 per cent to £2100 per annum (from £2000), you will now see that the profit has risen from £400 per year to a massive £735 per year, an increase in net profits of over 83 per cent.

If you now add new customers, whilst retaining the existing ones, the multiplier effect will become even more impressive. If you simply replace your hard-won customers with new ones, in other words your retention rate falls, the costs of selling *increase* far faster. This has the effect of wiping out large chunks of profit that would otherwise have been banked in the business.

controlling the business

So, how do you increase the customer retention rate? Well, we believe that this is a matter for your business in your marketplace, as every situation is different. In our business, however, we embarked upon a customer care project and appointed a customer care manager when no one else in the computer market was bothering. The effect was dramatic. The customer had about four times the previous contact level; we actively asked the customers if they were experiencing any problems with our products or service, and then went about fixing the issues, and telling the customer what we had done. In many cases, our sales increased in these accounts because the customer liked what we did, and the way we communicated with him.

There is one aspect of customer retention that crosses all boundaries of market sector, product and geography, and that is:

> *Make sure that your customer feels special all of the time, not just when he has an order to place.*

Simple as that!

Summary

We hope that this section has dispelled some of the misinformation and apparent complexity about sales and marketing. It is not a subject to avoid, it is the backbone of your business, and to truly succeed, it is something that you as a business leader will have to get to understand. We firmly recommend that you yourself attend a sales training course, as these are invaluable life skills that will repay your investment many times over.

In the marketing sections, we have tried to give you a concept of the possibilities. Marketing is for all companies, and not just the larger ones, and the key message here is simple.

> *Using technology and innovation, you can market just as effectively as the very largest of your competitors, and probably for a very much-reduced budget.*

We now invite you to be creative, and consider all of the different ways that you can market and sell to prospective customers in the future. Notice that we say 'all the different ways', as you must consider that your business needs many legs to stand on.

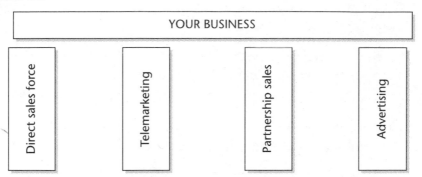

If your business has four legs of marketing, for instance, how much more stable is it than the business with just one leg?

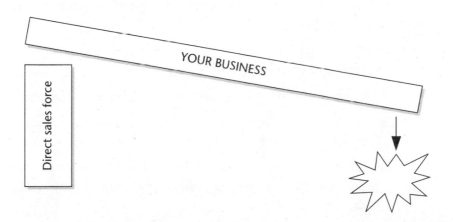

Your task now is to write the marketing plan for your company. Be creative and non-conformist. Never copy the competition; always try to go one better and innovate. The way that you write this plan may just spawn the idea for your industry that is equivalent to the first furniture store to offer crazy credit within their stores. It paved the way for massive profit increases and a healthy sales line in what was the early 1990s recession.

Will your business become an also-ran, or will it lead the way in a new and exciting way? The choice is now yours.

controlling the business

PRACTICAL STEPS

- Do not delegate responsibility of your sales activities – always keep your eye on the sales ball.

- Understand the various measurements for sales and use this information to increase sales.

- Structure the correct salesforce for the best results. Understand the 'pluses' and the 'minuses' of each option.

- Measure your sales and sales staff effectively.

- Qualify your sales opportunities by completing the relevant questionnaire for every prospective sale.

- Make every employee a sales person, no matter what his or her function.

- Operate a well-planned commision programme which benefits the company as well as the salesperson.

- Understand the power of purchasing and use all functions to leverage the best savings.

- Ensure you meet your sales objectives, and if you don't have any, write and plan your targets now.

- Analyze the checklist if sales do not come in as planned.

- Understand your Unique Selling Proposition and tell the world about it.

- Retain your customer at all costs and increase sales turnover by increasing the order frequency, order values and number of customers.

- Write the marketing plan for your company. Be creative and non-

the employment of staff

Recruitment of winners

The new starter

The time comes in any business when you have to make the decision to take on another helping hand and when the business is growing quickly the need can become urgent. Recruiting and managing new people in your business can become very daunting for any business owner. Will it help to run the business more profitably. What if the business cannot support the resource and suddenly you have to lose that person? Your decision does not just affect the business, but the individual who is out of employment.

The hardest lesson we had to learn quickly was the acknowledgement that you will lose members of staff, so expect it from day 1. Maybe they have only been there for a month, because they are not suitable for the position, or perhaps it's an employee who has been with the company for over a year but cannot meet the sales targets. Whatever the reason, you cannot hide from your responsibility of handling difficult situations which may lead you to ask an employee to leave your company.

> **You will lose members of staff.**

All managers and business owners alike hate this type of conflict and it can cause many a sleepless night but, as long as your decision is fair, honest and in the interest of the business's success then your decision can only be the right one. Managing people is probably the most frustrating task of all, as you are dealing with emotional beings and not a manufactured box!

Recruiting and managing people is something which, with the right processes and training, can make your life as a business manager so much easier. In the next two chapters we have included all the relevant documents, forms and training tips to make sure you are fully equipped in taking on human resource. Depending on the size of your business, you can adopt as few or as many of our suggested practices as you wish.

In this chapter we will cover:

■ advertising a vacancy

■ recruitment methods

■ interview process and forms

■ career path and interview/job analysis

- offer of employment, contract, staff handbook with model documents
- reference requests, medical and post-employment checks
- induction programme and training plan with model forms.

This chapter seeks to remove the uncertainty from the employment process, by providing the forms and relevant analysis documentation that is usually found in a larger organization. Use these forms and adapt them for your own use. Not only will it make your life easier, but it will also impress job applicants who are asked to fill your own in-house forms.

RECRUITMENT OF WINNERS

How to be a good manager

What makes a good manager? In our mind, becoming a good manager is something that cannot be achieved overnight nor taught in a week's course.

The technique for becoming a good manager is something that is influenced from the outside by gaining knowledge and experience in work situations, from books, qualifications, and life in general. This suggests a certain amount of time learning and maturing these influences. Training can assist your work knowledge and the chance to develop personal skills, such as presentation techniques, financial awareness and person-management styles. As you add to your knowledge and experience, you develop confidence to problem-solve effectively. This decisive approach creates the image of a 'good manager'.

Consider the model shown in Fig. 6.1 as an example of how your management abilities will grow by experience.

Advertising

There are five points to consider before advertising your vacancy:

- which paper/magazine to use
- who the readers are most likely to be, and whether they are the sort of applicants you want for the vacancy
- number of readers/circulation of the paper used. Must be a well-known paper with good image and circulation

- location of the paper/magazine
- your department budget for the advertisement.

Once you have decided on the above and are happy to continue, you will need to compose the wording of the advertisement. Opposite are two examples of advertisements for your information.

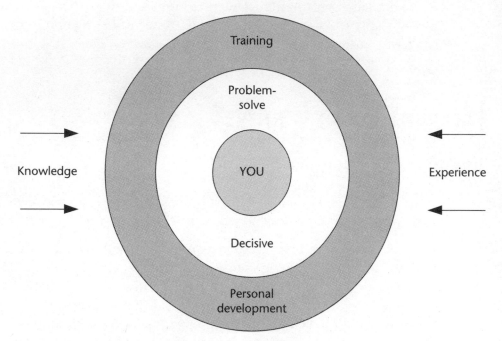

Fig. 6.1 THE GROWTH OF MANAGEMENT ABILITY

Please remember the following points.

- a short heading which indicates immediately to a reader the job on offer
- a paragraph about the type/character of the person you are looking for
- a paragraph on the skills, qualification and experience required
- the salary if desired (please check department plan)
- where to send the CV and to whom it should be addressed
- sentence on the company being an 'equal opportunities employer'
- if costed in the budget, include the company logo and any award insignias
- decide on the size of the advertisement. This is normally calculated centimetres down x number of columns across. Check the cost is in line with budget.

Two examples of advertisments

SAGE ACCOUNTS PROFESSIONAL

An experienced SAGE bookkeeper is urgently needed to run company accounts for a small but rapidly expanding IT company.

The right candidate must be competent with the SAGE accounts package. Duties will include: inputting all sales and purchase ledger payments and receipts, printing of management reports, compiling monthly VAT return and administering payroll PAYE scheme.

The position also includes dealing with the payment enquiries for suppliers, good communication skills are therefore essential. Other areas of budgeting and controlling expenses are involved, and therefore an innovative and willing approach is also required.

Promotion and salary package are excellent. If you are ready for a challenge and would like the chance to develop and create a new position, please call Mrs S. King on 0400-00333 now, or write enclosing your CV to:

Company address
An Equal Opportunities Employer

SALES CO-ORDINATOR

A mature, highly motivated and enthusiastic individual is sought to run and develop a sales support function within a small, but rapidly expanding, computer services company.

The successful applicant must have a minimum of 5 years' relevant business experience, be computer literate, and possess excellent communication and administration skills. Duties will include: order processing and fulfilment of customer sales, assisting the sales team, handling complex communication, buying equipment, developing systems, taking responsibility for problems and ensuring they are managed effectively, etc. Experience of managing junior staff is essential, as is the ability to excel in a fast, varied, and highly pressurized work environment.

Promotion and salary package are excellent. Please write and enclose your CV along with a short paragraph, describing the reasons why you feel you would be most suitable for this position, to Mrs S. King at:

Company name and address
An Equal Opportunities Employer

Recruitment consultants

■ Independent agencies

There are various agencies offering the service of recruiting staff on your behalf. The charge for this service is normally worked out on the salary of the person you need to employ. It can average between 10 to 15 per cent, sometimes it could be more.

In the *Yellow Pages* you can find details of recruitment agencies specializing in certain work areas, such as computers, accountancy, executive/managerial, distribution, secretarial and administration. These agencies can be used for temporary staff services in times of employee sickness or an increase in departmental workload. The cost is charged hourly, and can be anything between £5.80 to £7.00 per hour for a WP/secretary in the Midlands area to £12–£15 per hour in the London area.

The advantages of using recruitment agencies are:

- assistance in your recruitment. Can give the first interview and arrange interview tests on your behalf on their premises
- advice and expert information on marketplace
- they may advertise in local papers on your behalf
- immediate candidates on file
- if candidates are unsuitable, there is no charge.

■ Local government recruitment consultants (Job Centre)

Job Centres are very useful in giving advice on the general marketplace, and the salaries you can expect to pay for a particular position.

They also advertise the job on noticeboards to the public and details are kept on file. Please note that the general audience/catchment to these centres tend to be the young, unskilled/semi-skilled, and the lower-paid positions. If you have a vacancy for a junior post, this may be a good place to advertise and, of course, it is free of charge to the company.

■ DTI and TEC grants for new starter/training

Please call the local DTI advisor or local TEC before recruitment, as grants for training new staff may be available. You need to enquire at the time of recruitment, as the grants are not valid if the person has already started.

The interview process

Interview technique is not a difficult skill to acquire. Practice makes perfect, and if you have not had enough practice, work through the first and second interview steps (detailed on pp. 147 to 148) during the interview.

Interview preparation is essential.

If you are not happy with the calibre of applicants, do not recruit the 'best of the bunch'. Ensure your *full* criteria are met, even if it means waiting a little longer. It will save you precious management time in the longer term.

■ Interview preparation

Interview preparation is essential to ensure a smooth and organized interview. Make sure you have the following to hand:

- application form
- first/second interview tips (see later)
- psychometric test if you so choose
- written test scenario if required
- interview analysis/job analysis (form available on diskette)
- career path planning/personality profile summary (form available)
- job description (blank form available on diskette)
- company brochure/newsletter or any relevant documentation for the applicant to take away with them.

■ Application form

Please prepare yourself prior to interview. Ask all interviewees to complete the company application form prior to first interview. This ensures you have an accurate and full picture of the individual, free from the assumptions of a CV. [🖫 Application.doc]

To help you formalize your interviews, here is a checklist to follow for first interview and second interview.

FIRST INTERVIEW

Welcome
Shake hands, introduction, offer tea or coffee. Ensure the candidate has completed your company application form. If not, ask them to do so now.

controlling the business

Test

Set the applicant the psychometric test (if your company has chosen to operate this type of system), explaining how to complete it. Make sure they are happy and understand what they need to do. Leave them for an appropriate time.

Departmental/in-house test:

You may also like to give the applicant a test you have devised yourself, e.g. a test composing a letter or a typing test for a secretarial vacancy, to see how they communicate. You may like to give them a technical test if they are applying for an engineering post.

Application Form

Work through the application form and ask the candidate questions about it. This will help the candidate to feel comfortable and relaxed because you are asking them to talk about themselves, e.g. qualifications, work experience to date, skills they have acquired, where they live, married or single, children, etc. *Listen* and make notes on their answers.

The vacancy

Let the applicant have a short break, by explaining to them the job on offer and its responsibilities.

Question time

Ask all the queries you may have about the application form – why they left their previous positions, what they enjoyed in their previous jobs, particularly their present one. Ask what sort of manager they work well with, their strengths and weaknesses, where they see themselves in 5 years' time, what they want to achieve from their job. *What salary are they looking for in their next position? Listen* and make notes. Give the applicant chance to expand.

The company

Explain about your company, its marketplace and office environment. The company's ethos on team management, service, quality, etc. should be described. Inform them of how the vacancy has arisen.

Close

Ask the applicant if they have any questions; answer them. Thank him/her for coming along for the interview and say you will be in touch shortly. If you like, you can explain the interview process for the second interview. Shake hands.

Interview analysis sheet

Complete the interview analysis sheet (**⊞ Interview Analysis.Doc**) relating to the candidate and analyze the results with the in-house test. Compare these results with the career path summary and job description. Is the candidate capable of performing the duties? Have they had previous experience/relevant qualifications? Will they fit into the team/work environment? If you can answer yes to these three questions, bring them in for a second interview.

SECOND INTERVIEW

We recommend that there be an interview panel for second interviews. This should increase the chance of appointing the right person *first time*. The panel could consist of two or three representatives of your management – our panel would consist of three reps, you, your manager, and the senior secretary or whoever helps with personnel issues.

Welcome

'Nice to see you again', shake hands, tea/coffee.

The job

Remind the applicant about the position, work through the job description. Go through the objectives/goals of the job/department.

Questions

Ask the candidate what skills they think they can bring to the position, etc. Ask if they need any training to fulfil the job. Talk about areas of strengths and weaknesses (extracted information from in-house test or psychometric test if used). Suggest scenarios to see how they would tackle weaknesses. Search out information and experience. *Listen* to the answers. Give the applicant chance to expand. Make notes.

Company

Inform them of company performance review, motivation awards, commitment to training, health care, pension, etc.

Offer

It is recommended that you do not offer the position at the end of the second interview, as you will need to refer to the panel and confirm the decision together. However, you could arrange a tour of the building and whilst this is taking place a decision could be taken. If you agree the candidate is right for the job, you can offer the position. The wording would normally be: 'I am happy with the interview; your skills, qualifications and experience all fit in very well

147

with the position and, therefore, I would like to offer you the position of (job title), at a commencing salary of (£) with the next review in a year's time. This offer is given on the premise your references are satisfactory.'

The applicant may need time to think about it – tell them they can give you an answer in the next couple of days.

If they say 'yes', inform them of the probationary period, and that an offer letter together with contract of employment and staff handbook will be sent to them in the same day's post. Agree the start date.

Tour

Take the applicant around the office and show them around the various departments. Introduce the new starter if position accepted. Give them a company brochure and, if the applicant has accepted the job, give the job description and objectives to take away with them.

Close

Look forward to seeing them on start date or be in touch shortly after all applicants are interviewed. Shake hands.

Correspondence:

Send offer letter, contract of employment and staff handbook (*referred to later in this section*) or send a 'regret' letter for second interview. Send these out promptly.

Notes

Complete an interview job analysis sheet.

■ Correspondence

There are four standard letters to assist you in corresponding with applicants:

- inviting applicant for interview   (▮ Interview 1.doc)
- rejection before interview   (▮ Interview 2.doc)
- rejection after first interview   (▮ Interview 3.doc)
- rejection after second interview   (▮ Interview 4.doc)

Career path

We have spoken earlier in the chapter about developing and training staff, but to decide to implement a career path in the company is quite a commitment. We did include it in our company, but the importance of formalizing someone's career in your company has to be decided by you and your partners/board. Total commitment starting from the top down to all managers/supervisors will ensure success to this staff career programme. We have included information of how we included this information to help you decide if you would like to implement this into your staff development/planning.

> To implement a career path in the company is quite a commitment.

■ **Career path summary form**

The career path summary form should be attached to the job description *but* must be kept confidential and used to assist recruitment procedures and career path development for the position.

The form will show the calibre of person required to perform the job effectively, the qualification, skills and experience needed and the likely career progression in the company.

Please ensure the career path summary (■ **Career Path.doc**) is completed for each of your team members and kept in their personnel file.

Note: Senior management levels require up to 60 per cent skills in planning and forward thinking. Lower levels of management require 15–35 per cent skills in planning, forward-looking skills of estimating, organization design and finance.

■ **Job description**

Every employee must receive a job description to enable them to understand what their role involves on the day they join the company. It is useful to prepare this in advance, as it will assist you in the interview process. Please refer to Chapter 7, which details how to complete a job description.

controlling the business

CAREER PATH SUMMARY

Position: (Job title)	Company secretary	Reports to: (Job title)	Managing director
Job level: (bandings)	14–35	Benefits:	Health and pension schemes

1	Summary of duties
	The secretary's responsibilities are fundamentally to relate the corporate activities to Companies House in Cardiff and to perform the duties outlined in the Companies Act of 1985 modified by amendments in 1989.

2	Promotion to
	Company secretary experience leads indirectly to promotion upward to managing director and appointment to the main board as a director. Promotion to managing director must involve several moves beforehand: a move into sales, operations and then into business development while building up a proficiency in finance. Company secretary leads directly to a job enlargement of being a company secretary to more than one company.

3		Skills/experience and qualifications required
	(a)	Some skills in finance and accounting.
	(b)	Some skills in business planning, estimating and forecasting
	(c)	Interest and some knowledge *re* acquisitions and merger
	(d)	Familiar with electronics industry, specifically computer and software systems
	(e)	Ability to deal with personnel problems, and certainly from a legal point of view
	(f)	Company procedures and standards
	(g)	Knowledge of company law and Companies Act
	(h)	Knowledge of start-up of companies
	(i)	Reading in accounting, law, personnel administration, corporate finance, HNC or NVA in law or accounting.

4		Personal qualities
	(a)	Able to gain and hold respect
	(b)	Able to listen to company and employee problems
	(c)	Needs to be fair and firm when dealing with people
	(d)	Tolerant.

Testing and evaluation

■ **Written test**

Written tests are designed to test the applicant's ability to write a business communication. These tests would be suitable for secretarial/administration posts, for example. Special skills may also be tested, such as shorthand and typing.

■ **Psychometric test**

There has been much controversy about this subject whether it can, or cannot assist with the successful selection of your new staff. We can only refer to our experience and say that it can give you an indication of the employee's personality and what position they would do best in. However, whether the tests are completely reliable is never certain.

These tests should be used in conjunction with the other tips and forms suggested above and never in isolation. These tests can be very expensive and there are numerous private organizations which will operate these for you or train your management into conducting these for themselves.

■ **Interview analysis/job analysis**

This form (■ **Interview Analysis.doc**) is completed directly after the candidate's first interview. The interview analysis could be completed whilst the interview is taking place, ensuring the entries are kept private.

By reviewing the job description and career path summary, complete the job analysis. Fill in the first column and, after the interview, complete the second column. Analyze the form and use it to assist you in deciding whether to invite the candidate for a second interview. During the second interview, review and update the form if required.

controlling the business

THE NEW STARTER

Formal offer of employment

As soon as you have offered a position which has been accepted by an applicant, make sure you start a personnel file. These files should be available from a secretary and all company forms and procedures must be set out in this file for convenience.

■ Offer letter

The salary package is discussed informally during the selection process. The offer letter (■ **Offer Letter.doc**) confirms in writing:

- position
- salary
- holiday entitlement
- probationary period
- company health care scheme
- car/commission if appropriate
- hours of employment
- overtime
- commencement date
- name of reporting manager
- company requires three satisfactory references
- company requires satisfactory medical history record
- company requires the return of the signed contract of employment and sales and commission schedule (if applicable).

Our ref: (Company name)

Your ref: (Company address)

Date:

Dear

Re: (Job title)

I am pleased to confirm that you have been successful in your application for the above post and write to confirm the company's offer of employment.

Your salary at the commencement of your employment with the company will be £_____ per annum, payable monthly in arrears.

If you accept this offer of employment, your employment will commence on_____.
Please report to _____ at 9.00 am.

The 3 three months of your employment will be treated as a probationary period, during which time your employment may be terminated by us or by you on 1 week's notice. On satisfactory completion of the probationary period, you will become entitled to join the company's health care and pension schemes.

Your normal hours of work will be 9.00 am to 5.30 pm, Monday to Friday. Holiday entitlement will be 20 days per annum, five of which will be stipulated by the company.

The full terms and conditions of employment are set out in your contract of employment and the company's staff handbook. Please sign and return one copy of the contract and handbook to me, together with the completed medical history record.

The offer is subject to receipt by the company of the following:

- satisfactory references (unless you object, I shall contact the referees nominated on your application form immediately)

- completed medical history record

- signed contract of employment/staff handbook/sales commission statement (if applicable)

I look forward to receiving your acceptance and confirmation of your starting date. In the meantime, if you have any queries, please do not hesitate to telephone me.

Yours sincerely

cc: Accounts Department
          Personnel File

controlling the business

It cost us £300 to have our solicitor compose our company 'offer letter' and contract and we are happy to include it in the diskette for you, but do remember to get this checked by your own solicitor to ensure it relates to your own business practices (■ **Offer Letter.doc**). By having the new starter accept the offer in writing, the company ensures it can legally dismiss the employee if they have not satisfactorily completed the probationary period.

Note: One week's notice is required from either party to cancel the contract within the probationary period of 3 months.

This letter must be sent with the contract of employment (■ **Contract.doc**) and staff handbook (■ **Staff Handbook.doc**). Again, these documents should be checked and altered to fit into your own business organization and written in your own business style.

■ Contract of employment

The offer letter on its own is now not legally binding. It simply informs the employee that an offer of employment exists under certain conditions and explains in detail the package and conditions. It refers to the staff handbook for the regulations and standards expected by the company.

> **The offer letter on its own is now not legally binding.**

Two copies of the contract of employment are sent out with the offer and a signed copy returned to you for placing on the employee's file.

> *Please check the details on the contract very carefully to ensure clauses that are not relevant to the position are marked 'Not Applicable' e.g. provision of a company car.*

■ Staff handbook

The offer letter is attached to the contract of employment and the staff handbook. Together they constitute the *full, and legally binding, contract of employment*. Ensure a copy of the staff handbook is filed on the personnel file, as contracts may be amended in the future.

The staff handbook details precisely the company's regulations and procedures expected from its employees. It is important for the manager, as well as the new employee, to clearly understand these standards. Managers should read these regulations and administer them correctly and fairly.

■ **Sales and commmission schedule**

This schedule (■ **Sales Schedule.doc**) is sent out to all sales people to confirm the *variable terms*, which include sales target, commission scheme and assigned territory. The schedule is attached to the offer and contract of employment. The original should be kept on the personnel file and copies issued to the manager and employee for their own personal records.

See Chapter 5: 'Sales and marketing strategies', for tips on how to set up a commission scheme for your business.

Pre-employment checks

■ **Reference request**

Once you receive the offer letter complete with three references, check that these coincide with the employment history detailed in the candidate's application form.

*Call the referees personally on the day the applicant confirms acceptance and fill the reference forms out yourself (■ **ReferenceForm.doc**). This is standard personnel practice but you will need to seek approval from the applicant first. If, however, this is not possible, send out the reference forms immediately.*

Ensure you receive these forms back, satisfactorily completed. If you are not sure about a reference, contact the referee personally, saying all information is taken in strict confidence. Ask for more detail about the applicant's quality of work and attitude.

If you are still not satisfied, speak to the new starter and consult your managers. Agree if you should continue with the recruitment of the individual. If the person has already commenced their employment with the company and you are not satisfied with their work, the probationary period will cover the company legally and 1 week's notice should be given.

■ **Medical history record**

The medical history questionnaire will be sent with the offer letter (■ **Medical History.doc**) and should be returned by the new starter prior to his/her commencement date.

A company medical can be set up for any new starter if deemed necessary. The contents of the form will assist you in coming to this decision. Call to arrange an appointment with the company doctor (if you do not have one, ask your own doctor if he would be able to offer this service, which will be charged to the company). Once you are satisfied with the medical and references, place documentation on the personnel file.

If at any time during the employee's employment with the company, the information at the time of completing the medical history form was false or withheld, the company has the right to terminate employment immediately.

Post-employment checks

■ Extension of probationary period

If for any reason you are not completely satisfied with your new starter's performance at the end of the probationary period, you may extend the period for another month. You should do this in writing. However, if the new starter is not working to the standards expected, it is recommended the manager should terminate the employment at the end of the first 3 months.

■ Completion of probationary period

As soon as the probation period has been successfully passed, the new employee will be placed on the company's pension and health care schemes if you have them in operation.

Induction

■ Induction programme

On the first day, your employee will need to be briefed on company procedures and requirements as well as the job function. The induction programme will ensure your new starter is introduced into the company in a formal and professional way allowing all joining criteria to be met.

The induction programme also assists the reporting manager to have a detailed training plan for the first month of their new starter's employment.

Please see the induction programme attached (■ Induction.doc) and new starter details (■ New Starter.doc), which should be completed during the induction process by the manager. It covers all personal details, which must be copied to accounts department without delay, the original being placed on the employee's personnel file.

■ **Training plan**

The training plan (■ **Training Plan.doc**) can simply be handwritten and passed to the secretary for typing. An example has been included for your information and will help with the layout of the plan.

The training plan ensures that the employee receives a good introduction into the company and allows a smoother and more organised transition into the job. It also allows the employee to work towards targets and for you to measure their achievements and identify any weak areas that may need extra training. Review the first month on a daily basis with the employee.

Targets and training for the second month, etc. can be briefer and reviewed once a week.

During the third month, you should review the employee twice. Allow the employee to come to you with problems/queries. For the rest of the employment, continue to train and stretch all of your subordinates.

Problem solving

Ask your staff to come with a solution to a problem before they approach you for advice. Or, get them to work out a problem in front of you, by asking him/her how they would deal with it. If you are happy with their problem-solving, praise them. If they still need help in finding the right

> Your team member will start to develop their own answers.

answer, guide them, by prompting a suggestion. Let them think about it and talk out a scenario in front of you. Do not tell them the answer; you must let them work it out for themselves.

By using the above technique, your team member will start to develop their own answers before approaching you. They will eventually build on the experience and provide their own solutions to the normal day-to-day business crises. It will also improve the subordinate's confidence, as they will develop an insight and decisiveness when handling difficult situations.

controlling the business

TRAINING PLAN

Name:		Position:	PA to directors	Date of issue:	22.05.95

Date	Subject	Method of delivery	Objective
Month 1	Induction		Complete induction training within 2 days
	Meetings		Take meetings as follows, in no particular order:
			• Finance director (finance function and requirements)
			• Sales director (product, market place, futures and requirements)
			• Ops manager, process, access management reports, ISO9002
			• Sales manager, overview of Webb International business – your direct report
			• Managing director (corporation overview, development plans, new building, and forthcoming events)
			Overview filing systems of the company
	Filing Home Office		Visit MD office at home to control the environment and filing processes

TRAINING PLAN

| Name: | | Position: | PA to directors | Date of issue: | 22.05.95 |

Date	Subject	Method of delivery	Objective
Month 2	Environment		Change any control environments as necessary
	Process		Understand the processes of the company
	Company history		Meet with MD and describe in detail the company history and USPs
			Undertake financial training by MD or FD
Month 3	TAM		Review the *TAM Manual* and *Manager's Handbook*
	New building		Assist MD in planning new building layout
	Training		Formal review with MD to discuss future training

PRACTICAL STEPS

Four steps to ensure that you and your team tackle problems head-on:

■ *Question 1: What is the problem?*

Write out the facts. Half the problem in business is caused by people trying to make decisions before they have sufficient knowledge on which to base a decision.

■ *Question 2: What is the cause of the problem?*

Establish what lies at the root of the problem – discuss and write it down.

■ *Question 3: What are all possible solutions to the problem?*

Study the facts. Check past records, if appropriate. Understand consequences of the solutions.

■ *Question 4: What solution do you suggest?*

Write down the recommendation and act on it *immediately*. Get busy carrying out your decision.

If your employee needs further training by yourself, continue a new training plan for the next few months. You may need to send your employee off-site to gain more relevant training or to go on a course (please refer to the training section of this handbook).

managing people

Setting standards to improve performance
using 'SMART' technique

Job description

Objectives

Progress record

Annual performance review

Salary and job grading/career pointing

Disciplinary action

Resignation

The hardest part of all is the art of managing people.

Why is it that when you meet a group of business people in a room and you start to have a real heart-to-heart conversation with them, their biggest issue in the running of their business is invariably to do with the management of their employees?

> **Entrepreneurs find it hard to let go of responsibility.**

Why is this? It is true to say that the characteristics of a business leader or entrepreneur means that they shape their business and change direction for the best possible outcome, and so the pressure upon their employees is probably greater than in, say, a larger more established business. In addition, entrepreneurs can find it hard to let go of responsibility and therefore it is difficult for them to find a person with the ability to meet their high standards, and/or to find someone that they are comfortable working with.

When we started to employ people in our computer services company we were concerned about two things:

■ loyalty

■ commitment to our company.

We always felt that, if we had these two things, the fact that the employee did not have the relevant experience did not matter as we believed we could train that person into the position. Having employees with the right attitude was very important to us. We wanted to trust them and have a healthy long-term relationship with all of our staff.

It helped us greatly coming from a blue-chip background, because we were familiar with objective setting, job descriptions and performance appraisals. We introduced the latter immediately with our first employee. He was employed as a sales executive with no relevant sales experience but had the right attitude and bags of enthusiasm. As he was our first employee, and our intentions were to grow and develop him into a director of the business, we planned out a 6-month training programme to ensure he was equipped with all the relevant material and information to ensure he was successfully up and running, bringing in sales as fast as possible.

It worked, and after 3 months he was covering his own salary and bringing in a small profit, which increased steadily as he developed his product knowledge.

> *Three tips to training your employee:*
>
> *1 one training meeting per week and a progress review at the end of the month*
>
> *2 continually focus their time in ensuring they achieve their objectives*
>
> *3 support them and reward their efforts.*

Please note Chapter 6, which covers how to prepare a training plan.

When our first sales executive made his first sale, we rewarded him with a bottle of champagne to celebrate and, when we grew to 30 employees we had developed formal incentive schemes and a quarterly company award scheme. Even when we were £6 million big, we still made a point of a celebrating the first sale of a new employee.

Some of you may say that you do not possibly have the time to implement such systems and it is ridiculous in a small company structure. We acknowledge such opinions, as any systems that you introduce must sit comfortably with the leader; however, we performed an experiment later in our business to discover if spending time on appraisals versus leaving the employee to their own time management was justifiable. We were not surprised to find that an employee who is continually assessed and reviewed meets his or her job function and normally excels far more than someone who does not. The person who is left unreviewed tends to work less effectively in their job function.

Time is precious to any entrepreneur.

There is no right or wrong way of managing people.

Why is that? Probably one of the most crucial things we learnt with people and in social life is that people want to feel they are 'important'. By holding a formalized meeting every month to talk to them about their objectives, and how they are getting on, makes him/her feel that they are important to the company. And they are.

There is no right or wrong way of managing people. There is the formal approach, which we took, and this is set out in detail later in this chapter. Or there is the informal approach, where employees are left to do a job with

controlling the business

informal meetings and general overseeing as and when it is required. Time is precious to any entrepreneur and maybe the forms we have included in the diskette may help to make informal meetings a little more focused without having to spend the time on the full-blown appraisal approach.

Having a formal approach can help you to discipline your staff correctly and we will go into more detail later in the chapter. In disciplining staff there is an art to achieving the right balance without creating a negative working atmosphere. We received our 'Investors in People' award for our approach to our employees and some of these forms are on the diskette included in the book.

But please note: all that matters to your company is sales and making profits. If you are doing so without systems in place, great, carry on, but if you are having difficulty with employees, e.g. getting them motivated or achieving targets, a more formal approach may help you, particularly as you grow bigger in size.

We will include in this chapter the performance appraisal system which will include:

- setting standards by using the SMART technique
- objectives and progress records
- annual performance review
- disciplinary procedures
- incentive programmes and company awards

SETTING STANDARDS TO IMPROVE PERFORMANCE USING 'SMART' TECHNIQUE

The task

There is a saying which goes something like this: 'If you don't know where you are going, any road will take you there'. In order to focus our efforts productively, we must know what we want to achieve. A technique to help us do this is to turn our objectives into 'SMART' objectives.

The team

Since no manager can achieve the objectives alone, they need to ensure that the team is united in achieving the same objective. The fundamental questions to be asked are:

- what is the team particularly strong at?
- who has particular strengths?
- what areas of weakness do we have?
- where do I need to spend time in developing the team?

> Each individual has a particular role to play.

The individual

Each individual has a particular role to play within the team. Their main function may be sales, customer liaison, administrative support, etc. Just as the *team* needs SMART objectives, so the *individual* needs SMART objectives to focus their activity. These are derived from the objectives of the department/team.

The main role of the manager is to keep all the individual objectives together. If he takes one out, i.e. concentrates on one for too long, the others begin to suffer (see Table 7.1).

Table 7.1

Type of Management	Result
Too task orientated	Poor people managers, workaholics
Too team orientated	Not focused on results, forgets individuals, 'indecisive'.
Too individual orientated	Seen as having favourites, no direction

Defining the standards

- **Establish** the standards. Know and understand the standards yourself.
- **Communicate** the standards. Make sure that everyone who needs to know a particular standard is aware of it. If you delegate this task, be sure that you verify its satisfactory completion.
- **Train** for the standards. Ensure that all staff concerned have the skills to carry out the work to the correct standard.
- **Maintain** the standards. If a standard is altered for any reason, make sure that everyone affected is properly informed.
- **Enforce** the standards. If everyone understands the standards and is trained and able to perform to the standard, there is a need to pursue every non-standard performance with care and rigour.

controlling the business

'SMART' technique (see Fig.7.1)

> Standards must be set in terms that the workforce can understand.

Standards must be set in terms that the workforce can understand. They should be set with the same care and rigour as business objectives. A useful way of remembering them is that they should be 'SMART':

Specific
Measurable
Agreed
Realistic
Timed

Specific. There must be no confusion about the objective. The manager and the employee should be aware of its implications, value and the effort required to achieve it.

Measurable. Using the ideas of quantity, quality, time and cost, the objective should be expressed in terms that are easily measured – *the measurement should be accessible to both parties*.

Agreed. The employee needs to 'own' the objective and feel some responsibility to achieve it. This requires some 'selling' activity by the manager.

Realistic. The target should be one that both parties feel is achievable.

Timed. There should be a clear understanding on the timescale for the objective.

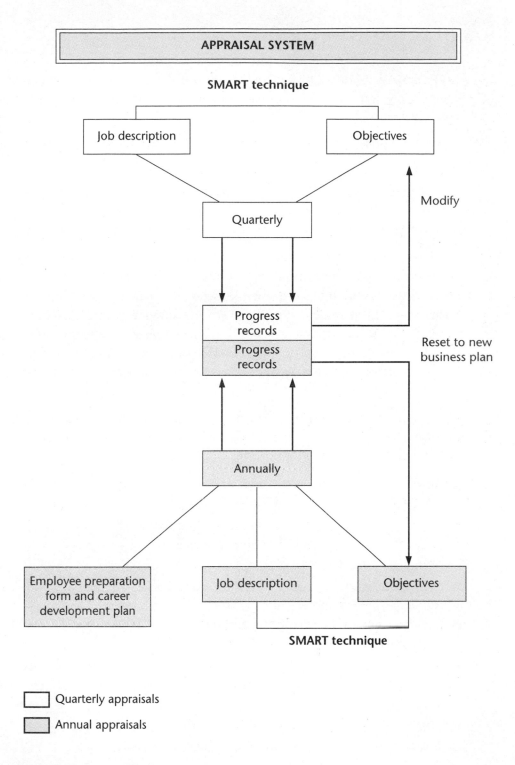

controlling the business

Fig. 7.1 APPRAISAL SYSTEM

JOB DESCRIPTION

Every employee should have a job description for the position. In the case of a newly created position, the reporting manager will need to design a job description.

A job description is a detailed description of the duties and tasks required for the position.

In the description of the task, you must include the standard/quality you require from it. *For example:* Ensure all telephone calls are handled promptly and in a professional, helpful manner. Use the SMART technique.

This will assist you in reviewing the employee's performance, and ensures no discrepancy in the standard expected from the task. It also ensures sensitive issues can be discussed openly in reviews. *For example:* your subordinate is very sharp and curt to callers. During a review with him/her, the job description can be used to indicate that a more pleasant telephone manner would show a more helpful approach to calls. It is a requirement from the job position and therefore cannot be construed as a personal attack on their character.

Please note: In our company job descriptions there were five mandatory requirements expected from all positions, and our managers ensured these were included in all job descriptions.

- **Appearance.** To be neat, tidy and of clean appearance in keeping with the company image.
- **Time keeping.** To strictly adhere to the hours of work outlined in the contract of employment and inform the manager of any sickness/holidays or time out immediately.
- **Behaviour and attitude to service excellence.** To deal with all customers, suppliers and members of the public in a happy, helpful and professional manner, ensuring the company image of service excellence and quality standards are portrayed at all times.
- **ISO9002.** To adhere to the procedures set down in the *Quality Manual for ISO9002*. To be continually aware and advise any members of staff who do not adhere to these regulations.
- **Clean desk policy.** To ensure the clean desk policy is strictly adhered to, and all confidential information is locked away each night.

Please see job description form (■ **Job Description.doc and Job Example.Doc**), which can be found on the diskette and completed by hand if preferred.

You will note there is a column marked PR. This stands for 'performance rating'.

During the employee's review you will discuss each task with your subordinate and inform him/her on their PR grade. (Please see performance reviews overleaf which outlines the 1–5 PR grading system.) As you review your subordinate, you will have established the 'average performance' rate from the job description by calculating the number of grades and agreeing on *one PR grade that consistently indicated the employee's performance to date. Place this final grade on their progress record, and in agreement with your subordinate.*

The objectives will also be reviewed in this way, and together with the job description, one PR will be agreed and placed on the Progress Record (■ **Progress Record.doc**)

JOB DESCRIPTION

Name:		Position:	Accounts manager	Date of issue:	

No.	Job description/task	PR
	Sage	
1	Input all suppliers' invoices correctly and post to correct department code. File hard copy invoice and place appropriate filing number on for easy retrieval.	
2	Input all company invoices correctly and post to correct sales code. Print off all invoices and send out and file.	
3	Input all receipts and payments accurately and post.	
4	Co-ordinate accurate management accounts as requested and report in company monthly meetings on status.	
	Payroll administration	
1	Ensure all salary administration is correctly entered into PAYE forms and accurately calculate each employee's salary. Keep a copy of each payslip advice.	
2	Ensure inland revenue summary sheets on TAX and NI are completed accurately and ensure inland revenue cheque is issued on time.	

JOB DESCRIPTION

Name:	Position:	Accounts manager	Date of issue:	

No.	Job description/task	PR
	Account administration	
1	Chase customer accounts for prompt payment. Type effective correspondence to ensure this happens refer to company models.	
2	Carry out accurate weekly cheque run for suppliers' invoices.	
3	Handle all invoice queries from customers/suppliers professionally and in a friendly, helpful manner.	
4	Pay in cheques to bank on time and accurately.	
5	Vet all applications for credit facility forms from our suppliers, and promote our purchasing power by increasing our credit facilities with them.	
6	Send and complete all credit facility forms from our suppliers and promote our purchasing power by increasing our credit facilities with them.	
7	Generally be aware of cash-flow position daily to enable effective functioning of sales and purchases.	
8	Set up BACS accounts and co-ordinate payments in a confidential and accurate manner.	
9	Liaise and develop a good relationship with the bank.	
10	Liaise effectively with sales co-ordinator and WP administrator to ensure all related problems which may affect sales functions are made aware.	
11	Handle and complete all paperwork involved for the international transmission of payments overseas, incoming and outgoing.	
12	Appearance.	
13.	Time keeping.	
14.	Behaviour and attitude to service excellence.	as stated under job description, p. 168.
15.	ISO 9002.	
16.	Clean desk policy.	

OBJECTIVES

What are they?

Objectives are a separate review process from that of a job description. A job description explains all the duties of the job position with the standard expected. Objectives work in line with the company business plan and goals.

The manager will review his/her department's annual development and planning requirements from the company business plan. The manager will then set objectives to meet the central goals and complete them by setting target dates. Please refer to the SMART technique to ensure objectives are set at the right standard.

These objectives are set annually and once the objectives are met for that year, they are replaced with the next year's strategic plan However, these may be modified during the year, if strategic direction changes take place. Any board directives should be added to employee's objectives. This will ensure they feel responsible for the process.

How to write an objective

One strategic plan from our business plan was to expand the human resource from one to four in the distribution department in the fiscal year 96/97. The objective was to be given to the appropriate manager.

	Objective	Target date
1	To plan, interview and recruit four distribution staff to handle the increase in sales turnover. Three junior and one functional manager to be taken on by target date. Plan to stagger recruitment over the year. **(H)**	By end third quarter
2	To design new job descriptions, training plan and objectives for the four new starters. To ensure continued training and review performance in line with company guidelines. **(H)**	In place by the time the new employees commence employment.
3	To organize new office layout to incorporate the four new employees and to purchase necessary office equipment/furniture within budget (H).	In place by the time the new employees commence employment.

Typically, this will translate as an objective from the manager to his/her subordinate as:

	Objective	Target date
1	To advertise, instruct recruitment consultants to identify potential candidates for distribution posts. Run first interviews. Present fair candidates for second interviews. (H)	End of June
2	Repeat Objective 1 in timescales indicated. (H)	End of September, December and March
3	To cost competitively the office equipment/furniture requirements for the new starters. (H)	End of June

In this instance, the manager has assumed responsibility for the job description, objectives, etc. and delegated the initial recruitment process to a competent subordinate.

Please note: This subordinate's objective shows a delegation of a generally junior level task and is not abdication of the Department Head's responsibility to fulfil the company objective.

Objectives can also include development work set by the manager which may not necessarily be detailed in the business plan.

Reviewing objectives

These actions are reviewed 3 months later and updated onto a new Objectives form (■ **Objectives.doc**). The objectives form can be typed but the 'Action to Date' column should be reviewed in the 3-month appraisal meeting and completed by hand when the actions are agreed at the meeting by both parties.

> **Objectives should be reviewed *every quarter*.**

> **Four objective forms copied on to the file over a year period will ensure a full picture is available of the employee's progress in the company.**

Objectives should be reviewed *every quarter* to ensure the company goals are met on time. The overall average grade for the objectives should be placed on the employee's Progress Record sheet.

controlling the business

Ensure each objective is categorized as:

H = high
M = medium
L = low

This level of importance will help the subordinate to prioritize his/her time for each objective.

The target date will work in line with that of the business plan. This is normally scheduled quarterly, i.e. end of fiscal Q1, which is end of the first quarter of your company year.

If you feel your employee is surpassing your requirement, you can offer some sort of achievement award to give further incentive on a continual basis. Refer to the incentive schemes detailed in chapter 5 of this book which details performance related schemes.

The job description and objectives will be given a final grade at the end-of-year performance review, and will form a direct relationship with the employee's salary increment for the next year. See p. 180 'How to grade' for further information.

At the annual performance review, ensure the employee preparation form and annual development plan (■ **Employee Prep.doc and Annual Development Plan.doc**) is completed. Review objectives, job description and the two preparation forms with your subordinate, completing agreed actions, future training and the PR grade during the review.

OBJECTIVES

| Name: | | Position: | | Accounts Manager | | Date of issue: |

Item No.	Objective	Level H/M/L	Target date	Action Date	PR
1	Update the company accounts on SAGE in line with business plan.	H	End Q2		
2	Implement new systems to all outstanding payments owed to the company quickly and ensuring all payments are received on time. Take the appropriate steps necessary to recover bad debts.	H	End Q1		
3	Handle all general account enquiries professionally and accurately.	H	End Q3		
4	Ensure and maintain cash-rich environment for the company and identify any variations.	H	End Q3		
5	Update and modify payroll administration efficiently and correctly and issue BACS on the last working day of each month.	H	By Q2		
6	Set up and organize the running of the accounts and finance department effectively to ensure the smooth running and an error-free system.	H	By Q2		

PROGRESS RECORD

Please complete this form (**Progress Record.doc**) *during* each quarterly review (see Fig.7.1). Ensure all your subordinates receive a copy of their progress record in order that they can check regularly for action points for improvement.

This form will assist you in measuring your subordinate's progress and ability to improve in their position. It should be completed after reviewing the job description duties and objectives. Information is then transferred on to the progress record form as a summary of all areas requiring improvement.

If urgent improvement is required, fill in an earlier date at Point No. 5 'The next review date' and check on their progress. See example of a completed progress record to help you complete these forms successfully.

PROGRESS RECORD

This form will be completed quarterly after each review to measure improvement and personal growth. A copy will be issued to the subordinate.

Name	A King	**Position**	Secretary
Last review date:	27 December 1995	**Today's date**	27 March 1994

1	**Actions required from last review**
	Improve telephone technique and manner (as outlined in last review) Organize workload to ensure high priority and urgent issues are completed first. Check all typed work for errors and ensure literature reads and flows well before signature. Ensure all filing is done promptly and correctly. Design new filing areas in line with sales department expansion.

2	**Progress to date**
	Improvement in telephone manner has increased, but calls still need to be dealt with more promptly. Do not keep callers waiting, transfer calls immediately and ask if you can help in the absence of myself. Errors still in typed work. Must improve immediately. Review in 2 weeks. All other areas satisfactorily completed – keep up the good work.

3	**Job Description PR**
5	**Objectives PR**

3	**Further areas requiring improvement**
	Poor attendance over last 3 months. Ensure you are in at work and ready to take calls by 9 am at the latest. Attitude to improve to all salesmen. Please make time for salesmen's queries. During busy times, ask politely if you can come back to them after you have completed the job you are on.

4	**Action or training to be taken**	
	Subject	**Timescale**
	No training required, though a typing certificate in advanced typing was discussed. This to be looked into during the summer to start in September at college. Improvement needed in the above actions points first.	

controlling the business

177

PROGRESS RECORD (continued)

5	Next review date
	Two weeks – 12 April 1994 and 27 June 1994
6	Additional comments

		4	Final performance rating

7	Employee's comments

Employee's Signature		Manager's Signature	
Date:		Date:	

ANNUAL PERFORMANCE REVIEW

At the annual performance review, complete the progress record after the review on your subordinate's job description and objectives. Summarize the year's performance with the PR grade (the agreed grade will be marked on the progress record, *during* the review). Now review the employee preparation form and annual development plan.

Note: Our company completed an annual review only after the employee had completed his/her fourth quarterly review. Salaries were therefore increased at varying times in the year.

Employee preparation form

Prior to the time of your subordinate's annual performance review, ask them to complete and return this form to you ▉ [**Employee Prep.doc**]. The information contained on this form can stimulate a discussion during the review and can also assist you in incorporating new objectives/development/training for the subordinate in the new fiscal year.

Annual development plan

During the employee's annual review, a quarterly progress record form will be completed. To ensure the employee's development plan is also reviewed, please complete the annual development plan ▉ (**Annual Development Plan.doc**). Use this plan as a basis for discussion of their future within the company. The employee preparation form will be discussed whilst completing this form and allows an agreed career path to be planned for the next year(s). (Review Fig 7.1 on p. 167.)

Performance review – how to grade

During the performance review, either quarterly or annually, the subordinate will need to be graded on the job description and objectives.

HOW TO GRADE PERFORMANCE RATINGS

PERFORMANCE RATING	CATEGORY
1	**EXCEPTIONAL** Continually surpassed standard required. No further room for improvement. (Please use sparingly, this grade denotes promotion.)
2	**EXCELLENT** Excelled in most areas. Frequently surpassed standards set. Some room for further development.
3	**GOOD** Good in most areas. Met standards requested and occasionally exceeded. Room for further development.
4	**SATISFACTORY** Did not fail or exceed in this area. Improvement required. This grade is normally used for employees with less than 6 months' service.
5	**UNSATISFACTORY** Unsatisfactory performance in this area. Three months' written action plan should be issued to the employee. Reviewed monthly. Failure to meet requirements will result in disciplinary action.

Job description and objectives are reviewed in detail with action plan/comment on each task and objective set. Employee should be marked with a PR set against each objective/duty according to achievement. Please see above for our standard numbering system.

Calculate each area measured to form an average review rating which will be agreed with the subordinate and placed on the progress record.

Please remember that when you come to grading your subordinate, the following guidelines apply.

The set of objectives/job description duties given to the subordinate represent the minimum standard required. If your subordinate achieves this standard, he/she should be graded a *Level 4*. Work that is done above that of his stated objectives and job description will qualify him/her to receive a higher grade.

In summary, a *Grade 4* is normal and acceptable and a *Grade 2* is considered excellent.

> **Do not give any grades away, grades are earned.**

Any year-end bonus and salary increase can be calculated using this performance rating.

During the annual review, objectives will need to be reset and agreed with the employee. This will include any areas which the employee has expressed an interest in developing. Please obtain sign-off at director level to agree the resources necessary to meet the development plan.

SALARY AND JOB GRADING/CAREER POINTING

If salary increment translates into a job level increase, inform your employee in writing.

If an employee is approaching career point by salary increment, but does not satisfy the criteria for career advancement, please refer to your manager immediately. This is a serious management issue for the company.

It is the manager's responsibility to develop their subordinate's career path in the company. At a career point, the individual must have had the appropriate career development prior to the increment to move him/her into a position of greater responsibility.

Try the following forms and charts to develop your own salary and career pointing structure that works for your own business.

controlling the business

JOB LEVEL BANDINGS

DIRECTORS

Managing Director 56
Financial Director
Sales Director
Operations Director
Business Development Director
Purchasing Director
Company secretary
Non-exec Director

Managers
Sales manager
Purchasing manager
Operations manager
Business development manager
Accounts manager
Software manager
Engineering manager
Distribution manager
Help desk manager

Supervisors
Sales co-ordination supervisor
Secretarial supervisor
Engineering supervisor
Warehouse supervisor
Accounts supervisor

FUNCTIONAL

(Revenue)
Sales (hardware)
Sales (software)
Sales (contract)

(Non-revenue)
Secretarial
Sales co-ordinators
Buyers
Warehouse co-ordinators
PA to directors
Receptionist
Accounts

Junior assistants
Secretarial
Warehouse
Office/administration

Bandings 10–65

60–65	Chairman
56–65	Managing Director
47–58	Functional directors
32–54	Management/non-executive directors
26–40	Supervisory
20–48	Functional – revenue earning
14–40	Functional – non-revenue earning
10–13	Junior functional

CAREER POINTING

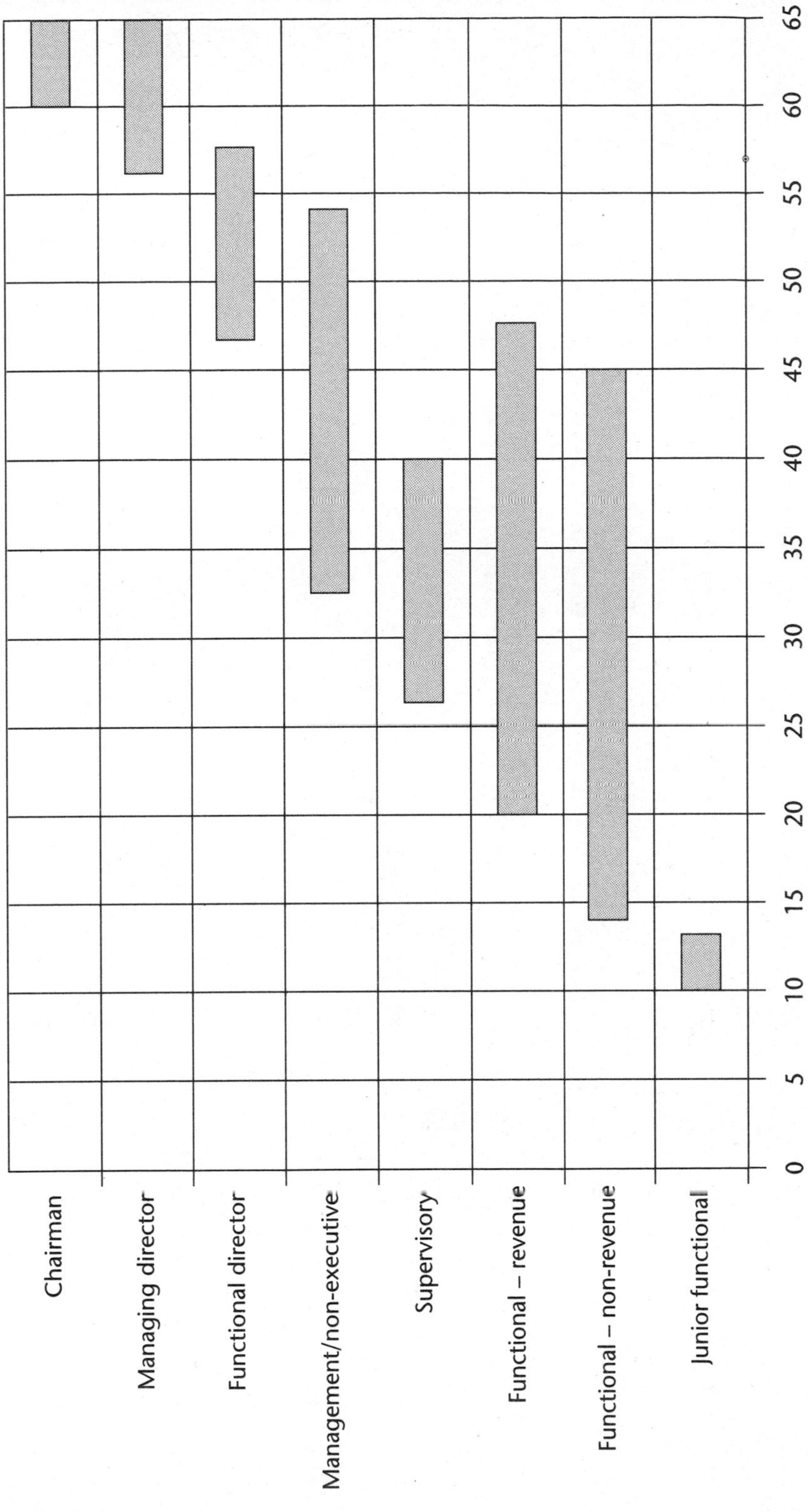

SALARY GRADING

Grade	Amount
10	£ 1,000
12	
14	
16	
18	
20	
22	
24	
26	
28	£2,000
30	
32	
34	
36	
38	
40	£3,000
42	
44	
46	
48	
50	
52	
54	
56	£5,000
58	
60	
62	
64	
65	£10,000

Potential salary increase
by two methods

- Promotion to higher job level
- Remuneration gained for annual
  performance review as follows:

Grade	Increase (%)
1	6
2	4
3	3
4	2
5	0

As salaries vary regionally and industry to industry, take the entry level job (10) and multiply 1,000 to what would be payable in your industry and region. Take the same multiples and create your own salary levels for each of the job grades 10–65. We have offered you stage multipliers as an indicator.

DISCIPLINARY ACTION

In the event of disciplinary action, follow your company guidelines, which may be assisted by a solicitor.

It is very important you keep all documentary proof of all conversations and written letters to hand in case the matter goes as far as a dismissal, which may in turn be taken by the dismissed employee to tribunal.

Always detail requests for improvement in writing to the employee and keep a copy in their personnel file. Remember, if you need support or advice, ask another member of management to be involved in the disciplinary meeting as a witness. Your employee is also entitled to a witness if he so wishes.

> Keep documentary proof of all conversations.

Progressive disciplinary procedures to protect your company

- Give a verbal warning
- Give first written warning
- Give final written warning
- Suspend pending investigation
- Dismiss.

It is so important to keep all information on your employee to make sure it's not your word against an employee:

1 Establish clear, written behaviour standards in line with your company policy and employee handbook.
2 Clearly communicate these to the employee and minute the meeting yourself or, if required, ask a witness.
3 Keep an action log of their progress and review each week.
4 If the behaviour or problem does persist, go on to the next procedure of written warning.
5 It is important that, if it continues, rather than dismissing on the spot, you give yourself and the employee a cooling-off period by suspending him immediately until further notice.
6 Keep a record of witness statements immediately so that you ensure the facts are correct on the day.

controlling the business

7 Remember to be like a detective and gather all information in the case of a dismissal. Interview and dismiss if the decision has been made to do so. Seek advice from a solicitor.

■ Matters to be considered before dismissal

- ■ One-year rule (currently subject to revision)
- ■ Valid reason
- ■ Have proper disciplinary procedures been followed?
- ■ Have recommendation of codes of practice been followed?
- ■ Investigation of events – dismissal before or after
- ■ Sufficient evidence to supply written reasons
- ■ Payments in lieu of notice or requirement to work notice paid
- ■ Cooling-off period allowed.
- ■ Have you reacted unreasonably?
- ■ Have you placed employee under unreasonable pressure?
- ■ Have you invaded the employee's privacy?

■ Discrimination-protected groups

Be aware of employees' rights from the following:

- ■ Race (Race Relations Act 1976)
- ■ Sex and marital status (Sex Discrimination Act 1975)
- ■ Pay (Equal Pay Act 1970)
- ■ Previous offences (Rehabilitation of Offenders Act of 1974)

If you are planning to issue a verbal rebuff, or indeed an official warning, ensure that you do not do this in front of other employees. Take the individual into a closed office or a private area in order to pursue this line of action.

Verbal warnings tend to be less formal and it is enough for the immediate manager to deal with their subordinate on their own at this early stage. If an issue becomes very urgent, contact your company solicitor for advice on employment law. The company will, of course, be charged for any advice given in these circumstances.

If you are unsure of how to manage the communications in a disciplinary meeting, a good technique to use is the 'I-Language'. Say what needs to be said!

- describe the other person's behaviour
- describe the effects of the behaviour
- describe your expectations
- describe the consequences if there is no change in behaviour.

EXERCISE

Use the method of I-language to assert your managerial influence when an employee is late for work:

When you _____

(an objective description of the employee's behaviour)

The effect is _____

(how the person's behaviour affects their performance or co-workers)

I expect _____

(factual definition of your performance and conduct expectations for them)

Consequences _____

_____

(a description of what the consequences will be if there is no change in behaviour)

_____

Example

When you arrive half an hour later than our normal work start time of 9 am, it *affects* the team because someone has to do your work as well as their own. It also *affects* the organization because customers are being told you are not available and we are not able to achieve our quick response call back targets. *I expect you* to come to work on time, every day. The *consequences of* not improving your time keeping will mean I will be forced to take further disciplinary action. This is a verbal warning.

RESIGNATION

In the event of one of your staff resigning, you will need to confirm the period of notice and inform your manager and the accounts department in writing, confirming the last day of employment with the company.

Prior to this, arrange an exit interview between yourself, your manager (if you request) and the employee. The aim of this meeting is to review the position, understand why the person has chosen to leave and see if there is anything the company could do to retain the employee's services, if appropriate to the circumstances.

It may be that there are career path openings in another department; an increase in salary may be considered, although new job responsibilities may have to go with this to align with the business plan and departmental objectives.

> **Wish them success in their new chosen career.**

If the employee is still intent on leaving after the exit interview has taken place, ask him/her to complete an exit interview form (▉ **Exit.doc**) in their own time.

Finally, have a short departmental meeting, inform your staff of the employee's decision to leave, express your sadness and wish them success in their new chosen career.

Summary

To help you with performance issues, we have put together some scenarios which demonstrate non-performance. Either in groups with your management team or on your own, discuss and formulate the following:

- the central issue
- evidence to the above
- the procedure you would use for tackling the problem
- your expectations using the I-language.

The 'I am right and everyone is wrong' guy

John works in distribution. He believes that he is doing a good job, and late deliveries are caused by the administration girls and nothing to do with his laziness in escalating delay in shipments. John feels that it is not his responsibility to remind the administration department, even though in his job description it outlines his responsibility to foresee late shipments and to anticipate them quickly and efficiently in order to ensure customer satisfaction. John has already received a verbal warning for his bad language to one of the administration girls and has now had a row with another administrator, who has blamed him for not informing her that a part shipment was over 3 weeks late. The girl is left crying because of John's rude comments. He is having marital problems at home and his work performance and interest in his job function has declined.

'I am doing my best, I can't do anything more ...'

Nicky has been in sales for over 3 years. She started with your company as a sales executive and has worked her way up to a manager responsible for the sales targets being achieved. Unfortunately, she has not met her targets for the last 3 months, her reason being that the marketplace is quiet, that there is no business out there and she cannot drum anymore business than she has already delivered. She is working 9–5.30pm, and her team seem very demotivated due to lack of sales. Nicky thinks it is a blip in the marketplace and after the summer it will get better. She does not seem concerned about the effects on the business due to low sales, maybe because she has been with the company for a long time and feels secure in her position.

Her objectives for the quarter state that she should meet certain sales targets which she has disappointedly not met and has consequently caused a large deficit in the company cash-flow.

'Sorry I'm late, I had a bad night ...'

Tony has once again arrived in late, moaning about having a bad night the night before. He has already turned up late twice in the last 2 weeks with other similar excuses. He works well during the day and leaves on time at the end of work. He is a likeable person and works well in the team; however, his colleagues are aware that nothing has been said about his late arrivals.

'Deceit and lies'

Jenny has been found with some stationery and diskettes in her handbag taken from the company stationery cupboard. The cost is approximately £50 to the company; however, it has been known that the stock cupboard has been short for the last 6 months. It cannot be proved it was Jenny and she defends herself by saying she was taking the items home to work on a project. Her manager was not asked by Jenny if she could take the items home.

'I only drink in my spare time ...'

Jim works very hard as a telemarketing manager running a small team of telesales people and meeting targets and objectives. His wife left him a year ago and he lives on his own. You have learned from one of his team that he likes a drink during his lunch hour and he has sometimes come in to work in the morning a little merry. You note these comments and make a point of occasionally dropping by to have a chat with Jim. One day he has come in with a small bottle of whisky in his pocket and his breath smells of whisky too. It is in your company manual and terms and conditions that alcohol is strictly forbidden on the premises and is an instant sackable offence. Jim says that he needs a drink in the morning sometimes to help him pick himself up and it won't happen again. He blames his personal problems.

controlling the business

I hope you enjoy running through these scenarios and that they give you the chance to role play effective handling of difficult situations. Remember, you have the final decision on all outcomes and, as you can see, personnel systems can back up these decisions.

PRACTICAL STEPS

- Set standards, use the SMART technique to write objectives and job descriptions.

- Ensure all staff have their performance reviewed at regular intervals and use whatever system suits your company. Make your staff feel important and they will want to perform better for you by the next review date.

- If your board agrees, increase salaries in line with your end of year company account profit figures.

- Include a disciplinary procedure in the company regulations and use these procedures correctly when necessary. Ensure all warnings are well documented.

staying afloat

how to control a growing business

Cash-flow management

Managing supergrowth can be compared to controlling the company rollercoaster!

So far in our book, we have talked about the basic ingredients, the essential lessons and the rules and ratios that are usually associated with growing a business. In the finance training module (Chapter 4) we suggested that a 10 per cent growth could be established with 100 per cent profit returned to the business year-on-year. But wait a minute, we have also been talking about our own business which grew from zero to over £6.5 million in just 4 years. With £100 share capital on the balance sheet, this represented a figure far in excess of 10 per cent growth.

So, if you are fortunate enough to have the product type, the marketplace or the niche idea, that takes you into the supergrowth category – *which is growth of 10 per cent or more* – what are the things you need to know, and what are the areas to pay attention to? The rulebook has just gone out of the window, now what?

Well, first of all, this chapter is relevant to most of you in the early years of business. In many cases, the small business will grow at astonishing rates in percentage terms, and although they may not get to £6.5 million in 4 years, the rate of growth can be life-threatening none the less. Most businesses fail with orders on the books, but no cash to keep the business alive.

This chapter will therefore cover all aspects of how to manage your growing company and includes:

■ how to create a cash-positive environment
■ understanding the needs of the growing business
■ factors to strengthen and overcome the difficulties of supergrowth.

In the sales and marketing chapter, we provided a checklist for a situation of low sales. We told you to liquidate stock as fast as possible in this event, as the cash-flow will be at its worst in the weeks to come, not at the precise moment when sales are low. We would like to offer you a list of activities that all have a direct bearing upon the *cash available* to the business, and you must pay daily attention to this list if you want to succeed in the super-growth league.

CASH-FLOW MANAGEMENT

Collection of debts

This may sound perfectly obvious, but so many businesses automatically agree to extend payment terms, or simply accept the lame excuse that the cheque run has been missed. The average debtor days (see 'Finance and accounting' for definition) should not exceed 48, if you want to survive in the supergrowth league. Focus the best person you can possibly find to look after this task. In our business, we employed an extremely tenacious, young and enthusiastic individual for this task. Her 'no nonsense, tell it

> We employed an extremely tenacious, but young and enthusiastic individual.

how it is' style made her few friends, but always gained a result when accounting departments tried to delay payment. In fact, she had little in the way of accounting qualifications, but she was absolutely right for the position, and our business would never have sustained supergrowth year on year, had this function not been correctly staffed.

> **Rule 1:** *Cash is absolute king.*

Retention of payments to suppliers – better terms

It's amazing how often you can ask for and get the right payment terms for your business. When your business is new, or recently established, the supplier likes to ask for cash up-front, or cheque with order. Instead of mumbling a form of agreement with their request, try suggesting that this arrangement is not good for continued business, and that you propose that a 35-day post-dated cheque be used in the first order, and a credit account for net 30 days be established thereafter. (Net 30 days means that you pay for the goods 30 days after the end of the month of delivery. If you take delivery on the 1st of the month, you will pay for it almost 60 days later.)

If you sound bullish enough, the deal is done. As you grow, your new supplier can be told that you simply never pay up-front, and that a net 30-day invoice arrangement is the *only* way to get your business.

Minimize the daily overheads

If you have been in business for a while, and particularly if you employ staff that have authority to spend or commit the company's money, it will be highly likely that your business may have overheads, costs or commitments that you might be well able to do without. To conserve the cash in your business, it is imperative that you control your purchases and points of purchase. Even if you and you alone control the company spend, there will be ways of saving money and therefore maximizing the cash available.

Consider this question: How much is a litre of petrol? It sounds simple, and if you know the answer, then we'll ask you another: How much is the cheapest litre of petrol, and do you buy your fuel at this garage every time you need to fill up? The reason we ask these questions is to illustrate the point that the variance between the cheapest litre and the most expensive litre is around 15 pence. If your car takes, say, 50 litres in a tank, that difference can be multiplied up to £7.50. If you use one tank per week, this becomes a huge total of £390 in a single year. If you run more than one car, or use more than one tank per week, this figure becomes a frightening total representing a complete and useless waste of cash.

We have shown you this simple illustration to underline the point made above. Every business must reduce and continue to contain overheads to maximize the cash available for working capital.

It is easier to save a pound than it is to go out and make one.

Have daily cash forecasts in place

By understanding the cash position in written form, and updating this daily, you will have a factual reminder of the available cash to the business. Even when our business was turning over £6 million, we still required a written cash position on a weekly basis, along with a week-by-week forecast of the bank position over the months to follow. Only by understanding this could we control the stock levels, and the authority to buy for stock. When cash became tight, the authority to buy for stock was removed; when cash was available, we maximized profits by spot purchasing.

Keep the stock to an absolute minimum

The stock in your business may vary from raw materials to general supplies or sub-components of your finished goods. By any other name, your stock is dead cash. View your stock holding at the same moment that you view your bank balance, as the two are very closely linked.

> Make sure your company never buys an item without checking the stock levels first.

> **Rule 2:** *Your stock is dead cash by any other name.*

In your supergrowth business, make sure that your stock turns regularly, and that any slow-moving items are liquidated for breakeven on a periodic basis. Liaise with your suppliers, as the reasons for your holding the stock as opposed to your supplier delivering on a just-in-time basis may have been forgotten over time, or simply not explored at all. Incentivize your sales team to clean out the stock items from time to time, and make absolutely sure that your company never buys an item without checking the existing stock levels first.

In our business, the rapid growth meant that our stock system recording and the accuracy of the data became less than perfect. There were many occasions where our operations staff purchased goods from suppliers even though the item was actually in our stock.

> **Rule 3:** *Your stock records are as important as your bank statements.*

Defer any pay rises

When times are hard in terms of cash flow, and your staff annual pay review looms over the horizon, it is tempting for the sake of retention of staff to simply award the pay rise as you would like to do. This action will exaggerate the cash shortfall every month that goes by, and you may wish to consider other means. It is not uncommon to have an open discussion with your staff member, and perhaps to find a way of deferring the pay rise until some months later. For example, your intended 5 per cent pay increase could be restructured to a 7 per cent rise but effective in 6 months' time. In this way, the award has been made, the employee remains motivated and loyal, and the business has reduced its overall cash outflow for the critical months.

Of course, there are other ways of making package increases. Consider the many elements that go towards making employees satisfied with the company that they work for: such factors as training, pension contributions, health care, parking spaces, and don't forget the employees' personal interests. All of the above can be paid to the employee without the business paying national insurance, although the issue of benefit in kind tax liability may be relevant in some of these cases.

Our advice is to be creative when you are growing a business and are faced with cash-sapping pay reviews. Consider the often forgotten national insurance gain by not awarding the package increase in gross salary, and make sure that your business can afford the pay review in the first place.

The characteristics of a supergrowth business, particularly when you have had a run of success, usually mean that your confidence of further high growth is boosted. You may fail to consider the possibility of a slow-down in growth, and as a consequence allow the overheads in terms of salaries to rise beyond a sensible level.

Be careful of using the promotion mechanism in a small business. The title award is a very powerful one, and can often give rise to confusion amongst staff, and loss of focus at a time when this is most needed.

> **Rule 4:** *Build as much flexibility into your salaries as possible to allow for periods when growth may slow, and profits may fall.*

Control the telephones and mobile phones

Particularly if you are a service business, it is likely that your telephone costs will represent a significant outlay in percentage terms. In our business, we would reassess the telephone systems and, more importantly, the service provider on an annual basis. As technology improves, the possibility of making large savings by using independent telecom carriers becomes common. See Chapter 11 for more about the effective use of technology.

This aspect can be considered under the point above, in which we talked about controlling your business overheads. The other point about control concerns the use of the telephone itself. Consider using the fax to set out complicated issues, rather than spending valuable time on the phone explaining them, or perhaps setting the fax machine to send out the daily or weekly faxshot to transmit after 6 pm instead of during the working day.

Mobile telephones can be a huge drain on company resources, and are often the emotional issue that no one likes to tackle. In a fast growth business, these loose ends drain cash faster than most, and must be tackled. All mobiles have a

> **Mobile telephones can be a huge drain on company resources.**

printout of the numbers used and the times of the calls, and asking the user to attach this printout with his/her expense claim is a good way of instigating a subtle control without causing a fuss.

Always look to increase working capital by finding new suppliers

In a supergrowth business the amount of operating cash that is available to the business must become a major preoccupation on a monthly basis. In our business, we regularly recontacted our suppliers and requested higher credit limits, whether or not we needed them at the time. In addition, we always had a practice of increasing the number of suppliers to our business, even if we did not use them often.

What was the point of this, you may ask? Well, it is quite simple. When the business grows rapidly, there will inevitably be a time when a customer payment fails to arrive on time, or a particularly large deal comes your way. Whether it be the positive or negative factor, the result will be the same.

You will suddenly find that you have insufficient cash to pay all of the suppliers that you should be paying if the world were perfect. When you find yourself in this position, you must have a back-up plan.

By increasing the credit limits as above, you may be able to still take supply for a few more days or weeks without it becoming evident to the supplier, as an exceeded credit limit is usually viewed more seriously than an overdue payment.

If this becomes difficult, and the supplier applies a stop to your account, then by adopting the many supplier approach above, your business will at least be able to continue to trade and purchase goods to sell, even it is not at the same preferential pricing as your normal supply route.

> **Rule 5:** *Most businesses fail because of the lack of operating capital available.*

controlling the business

Always project a higher overdraft facility at every bank review meeting

By assuming the exact same stance as above with the bank, you ensure that a continued overdraft review is expected. Based upon an increased turnover, you should expect to negotiate an increased facility by the judicious use of cash-flow forecasting.

This can become the lifeline to your business in times of hardship, and spending time with your bank, enabling them to gain an understanding and trust with you and your business will pay dividends in later times. If your bank fails to share the same enthusiasm for your business that you do, then change banks. In a supergrowth business you can ill afford the bank relationship to hold you back for no good reason. This may sound like a glib statement considering the amount of complex debits and standing orders that relate to your account. If you change banking relationships, you will find that all of these details can transfer almost seamlessly. In other words, your new bank will perform all of the set-up instructions on your behalf.

There may be significant pressures from the banking institutions to ask you to consider invoice discounting or factoring as an alternative to the straight-forward overdraft or fixed loan arrangements. Whilst these can be of huge benefit to some businesses, it may not be right for yours. Consult your accountant before you make these decisions, and understand the conditions by which you can terminate these arrangements in the future.

In Fig. 8.1 we have tried to show you the ideal model of satisfying the cash needs of a growing business. As the growth of the business curves upwards, this is supported by elements of fixed loan, leases or equity (share finance). The variable and what we could call the 'peak and trough' needs of the business should be satisfied by an overdraft facility. It would be a higher risk approach to finance the entire needs using an overdraft facility, as exposure to one lending source leaves little room for manoeuvre.

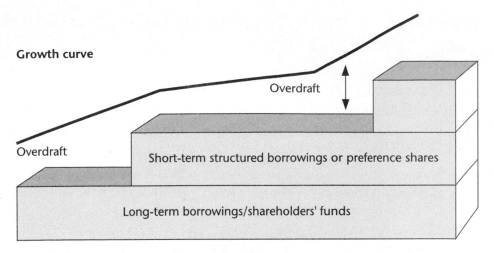

Fig. 8.1 CASH NEEDS OF THE GROWING BUSINESS

controlling the business

Use leases to retain cash, as opposed to purchasing assets

From time to time, your business will need to invest in assets such as plant and equipment or motor vehicles. Be aware of the different options available to you financially. Instead of tying up valuable cash which could be used elsewhere, look at the possibility of using a lease arrangement to fund the purchase. This way, you simply lay down a deposit, and commit to a repayment plan over a period of time. In some circumstances – using a rental plan, or an operating lease arrangement – you needn't end up owning the equipment at the end of the period. Again, consult your accountant for the advice relating to the various funding methods open to you, and our advice is to carefully consider any options that will maximize the cash to the growing business.

Sale and leaseback of existing assets

It may well be the case that you have been in business for some time, and that you already own assets for which you have paid cash. In our own business in our fifth year, we had around £30 000 worth of IT equipment, which was bought and paid for in cash. At one time when the cash was tight, we negotiated what is termed a sale and leaseback of this equipment.

This was the sale of the entire IT assets to a leasing company of choice for the same amount as was on the balance sheet. We then signed a lease agreement for the same IT equipment and entered into a structured repayment plan. The equipment did not, in fact, leave our building, and the operations of the business did not change. The net effect was that our business received a cheque for £30 000, and our payments became around £3000 per quarter. The prerequisite is that your balance sheet shows sufficient creditworthiness to sustain this financial transaction, as any leasing company will tell you.

Maintain the strongest balance sheet possible

In a small business, you will often be asked for copies of your accounts and balance sheets, to increase supplier credit or to support a large customer deal, which requires you to be vetted financially. This is likely to occur often in a high-growth business, and becomes very common in a supergrowth company.

> **Understand the factors that can affect the balance sheet.**

The rules of accounting, although well defined, are in fact open to interpretation with reference to an individual business. We advise you most strongly to understand, by working with your accountants, the various factors that can affect the balance sheet.

The most obvious factor is of course the profit and loss account. The decision of whether to maximize your profits for the business or to minimize them to reduce the taxation burden is a fine balancing act. You must be the judge of the effect on your own business, and the future position once your accounts are filed.

Other factors that can strengthen a balance sheet quite legitimately:

- The policy relating to depreciation of assets. If the depreciation is taken over, say, 5 years as opposed to, say, 3, the write-off to the profit and loss account will be reduced and therefore you will show higher profits.
- The treatment of assets generally if, for example, you group several low value items together and record them as assets rather than writing them off to the profit and loss account.
- The treatment of expenditure that is development work but will be used to make future profits. If you can prove this with a written plan, it is possible on some occasions to capitalize these as intangible assets. This will

have the effect of increasing profits, and strengthening total assets on the balance sheet.

■ Using rental equipment instead of purchasing or leasing will leave the costs to the monthly profit and loss, and will not show as a liability on your balance sheet.

There are other ways that are more complicated, and we leave for you to explore with your accountant. See Chapter 9: 'Legal and accounting' for more advice as to how to instruct your accountant.

> **Tip:** If your balance sheet for the last year does not show a strong position that supports your current trading aspirations, file this as late as possible with Companies House in order to reduce your exposure to those credit checkers unknown to you.

Management techniques

In a supergrowth business, the most critical factor that will affect your ability to survive is your management ability.

> In a supergrowth business the most critical factor is your management ability.

The needs of the business change so fast that you must almost run to keep up. Read Chapters 6 and 7 for in-depth guidance of how to manage people in a growth environment, but read on for a snapshot of the differences in style, which you must be aware of in a supergrowth business.

There is always, in any business, what we will call the core staff. These are the people who were there at the beginning, or close to the beginning. They are the individuals who will always remember you as one of the team, the person who started out driving the old second-hand car, and worked the business 24 hours a day.

As your business grows, you will employ more people, who will not become core staff. They will want to work for the company, and not for you. They may well work the numbers of hours for which they are paid, and want to go home at 5.30, for instance! The ability to recognize that this is not their weakness, and is something to be accepted, is often difficult. In a high-growth business, this can often become irksome, and the cause of stress for you. Our advice is that you understand this manifestation, and learn to control it, whilst keeping an eye to the core staff.

Retention of your staff is highly desirable in your growth business, as to lose people is going to cost you time and money in recruitment and training. In Chapters 6 and 7 we showed the performance measures that can be used to control, and discipline, staff in the event of non-performance. In our high-growth business, it became vital to recruit correctly first time, and so much so, that our management teams were all asked to take formal recruitment training to increase our chances of success.

> **When you grow your business do not promote the longest serving member**

The structure of your business will become very important on a quarterly basis as opposed to an annual one. Read the training module carefully in Chapter 4 to understand the stages of preparation that you can apply to the growing business. In our own business, we frequently reappraised our management lines, teams and focus of our business in order to maintain a positive environment for the staff to operate in during a sustained period of growth.

When you grow your business, it is critical that you do not succumb to the temptation to promote the longest-serving member in order to 'repay' the loyalty to your business. Too often, we have seen this happen and almost always it ends in tears. We made the same mistake in our own business, as we promoted our first employee to the dizzy heights of sales director, a role for which he was ill prepared.

The result was that he was handed a set of responsibilities that he could not hope to fulfil, the sales team perceived his dilemma and became less focused. The business suffered through lack of direction and we eventually had to ask him to step down, and allow the business to hire a professional external to the company to fulfil the role of sales director. It was fortunate for us that he was a true professional, who stayed with the business to work for the newly appointed sales director, and went on to become a successful salesman.

> **Rule 6:** *Always appoint the very best person for the role, regardless of whether he/she is external or internal.*

Control of the sales margins

In a period of high growth, it becomes very easy to simply look at the turnover growth and congratulate yourselves. During this time, very often the gross margin in percentage terms will fall, often very dramatically.

Our own business suffered a fall from the first year of 22 per cent to year three of around 14 per cent, despite a turnover increase from £200 000 to over £3 million. You may think that 14 per cent of £3 million is definitely better than 22 per cent of £200 000, but just think what could have been the outcome if we had managed to control our gross margins to around even, say, 18 per cent. The net profit to the business would have increased by £120 000.

For many reasons, often a simple case of euphoria, the margin percentage can fall, and the high-growth business is almost always affected. By highlighting this aspect for you, we hope that you can stem your gross margin decline, and pick up the resultant net profits that you justly deserve.

Eye to the breakeven point

This paragraph really pulls together the symptoms of a high-growth business that we have discussed above: the gross margin, the control of overheads, the careful assessment of the pay review strategy, the daily control of cash within the business. By definition of a growth business, there will be times when the sales do not ramp upwards in a linear fashion, despite all of your efforts and planning. We urge you to consider this point with care, and ensure that you maintain a vigilant approach to watching the sales to breakeven position.

We always knew to the almost exact figure what the next month's breakeven figure was going to be, and the magical sales numbers that would take us across that line into profit. See the financial training module in Chapter 4 for information about plotting your breakeven position.

Focus on the strategy

The high-growth business is synonymous to driving a racing car. The bends arrive so much quicker than normal, the engine revs faster, and the alertness of the driver is the key to potential success. When your business becomes fast-moving in this way, it is vital that you have a view of what is in front of you. The strategy of your business and the vision that you articulated in the

controlling the business

> **The strategy of your business will need to be reviewed regularly.**

opening chapters of this book will need to be reviewed regularly. A good perception of the marketplace and economic factors is needed as well as an 'ear to the ground' with respect to your suppliers and customers.

If you have not constructed the vision statement, you must define it without delay, and don't be afraid to return to it if the conditions change.

Resources versus profits

In earlier chapters we have discussed the growth potential of the business and suggested that a 100 per cent return of profits to the business can facilitate a 10 per cent growth model. In achieving supergrowth, you will have

> **Carefully plan your resource needs.**

taken note of all the factors regarding cash-flow and cash retention in the above sections. The next question is how much profit should you show (retained or otherwise), as opposed to expenditure on additional resources for the business. There is no prescriptive answer that we can give you, as this is particular to your own business. Obviously, you will be subject to a tax charge on profits declared, but the profitability may augur well for the extension of your credit lines and bank facilities.

The answer to this issue is, of course, a balance. You must generate sufficient profits to support your operating capital needs, both in current terms and also for the next financial year. If you continue to grow, this need will grow ever larger, and require a leveraging of the profit multiple to grow the credit lines. On the other hand, of course, is the need to resource the business in line with, but, we suggest, just behind the growth curve of the business. Often, this resource will show as assets that will not weaken the balance sheet simply by being moved from the cash pot to the fixed asset pot. However, if these become revenue items, profits will fall.

Carefully plan your resource needs, and plot the year-end dates to maximize your balance sheet worth. To some extent, you can manipulate your profit declaration through your accounting policies, as long as these policies do not change from year to year.

> **Rule 7:** *Resource your business marginally **behind** your growing needs.*

Factors inhibiting high growth

It may well be that you have not yet embarked upon a quest for growth, or that your business is struggling to find the growth factors to promote it to a larger entity.

Try the following list of possible causes. The answer to the issue identified will be found either in the sections above, or in the chapters relevant to the subject.

- The business has insufficient cash available.
- There is no stated vision to promote growth.
- The marketplace is not understood.
- The sales volume is low, or the customers are few in number.
- There are too few people selling.
- The whole company relies upon one man/woman.
- The use of effective IT in the business is low.
- The experience of the employees is low.
- The directors/owners have not undertaken financial training.
- There is no formal planning process in place.

There are other factors, of course, and the list is not exhaustive, but represents some of the common factors that prevent a business from achieving growth to the owners' satisfaction.

Remember that you are in control of your business, and the growth percentage does not have to be startlingly high as it was for us. If you grow at 10 per cent or more, then you can categorize yourself as a high-growth company, and will be extremely likely to experience some of the problems stated above.

Planning to stay alive – base plus development

In a growth business, particularly a high-growth small business, it is so easy to lose track of the marketplace which you were originally set up to address. Indeed, there are many good reasons why your marketplace must perpetually evolve in line with your customers' expectations, without losing sight of the origins of the business.

In the sales and marketing chapter, we discussed how many businesses lost track of the original set of customers, who were quite happy to continue to place orders with your business, if only a salesperson had continued to pay them attention.

In the planning section, we reviewed the concept of base business and development business, and the importance of defining and constantly measuring them separately.

In your supergrowth business, this exercise becomes even more important, as the time periods between major change are frighteningly short. The origin of this approach must lie in your sales budgeting at the start of each financial year, and then you must assume the discipline of reviewing it in the same way.

The results of this plan will be to show your business as it evolves, and will focus you and your staff upon keeping the base business alive, whilst developing new. This will have the effect of maximizing your profits at a time in your business life when they could so easily slip away, due to wastage and lack of clear focus.

In our own business we constantly fought to keep the focus upon the base and very profitable business, and set up separate operating divisions to handle the new development businesses. We even went as far as to create wholly owned subsidiary companies and formed a group structure in order to clarify the marketplaces within the business. Whilst this is not a recommendation, there is certainly merit in dividing the business in the areas of focus. Seek advice from your accountant before you embark upon group formations, as the tax treatment changes in this circumstance.

Board control

The final area in our 20-point (*See* pp. 269–70) examination of problems relating to fast-growing companies is the critical area of control. In Chapter 4: 'Training to stay alive', your company was represented by a raft. On this raft, the rudder was synonymous with the strength of the controlling managers and the board of directors. With the cash-flow represented by the keel of the raft, the situation of poor cash-flow, making for a small keel; would render the raft unstable, unless the rudder were large enough to cope as a keel, as well as a steering device.

> In supergrowth companies, the strength of the board or senior partners, is vital.

In our supergrowth companies, the strength of the board or senior partners is vital. If the board lacks clarity or doesn't understand finance well enough, your business may well be heading for the rocks, as our raft does in the above chapter on training.

Examine your board make-up for the following points:

- Board meetings are held monthly.
- All meetings are minuted accurately.
- The agenda is issued a week in advance.
- The company secretary is well versed in the Companies Act 1985/89.
- The directors are all aware of their fiduciary responsibilities in law.
- Monthly management accounts are prepared and examined.
- All directors understand how to read the profit and loss statement and balance sheet.
- Monthly cash-flow model is prepared.
- The board receives reports in detail from the following departments: sales and marketing, fulfilment department or manufacturing, accounts department, other vital function departments.
- The managing director prepares and submits a report to summarize the month past, and the month in hand.
- The use of non-executive directors or board advisors has been considered to add experience to the board from outside the business.
- The directors have all attended at least one external training course in the last 12 months.

If your board is lacking any more than one of the above, consider this list as an action list. The strength of your controlling board is vital to your success in a fast-moving and growing environ-

> **Your controlling board is vital to your success.**

ment, and your supergrowth business will undoubtedly benefit from this approach. The Institute of Directors in London run a series of excellent courses if you need further assistance in the areas of board-level training; the CBI has links to professional training organizations who would also be able to tailor courses for your particular needs.

Final point

Managing a company that is growing in excess of 10 per cent per annum is commonplace for the small start-up business, but all of the normal points of business advice are geared towards the 'normal growth' company.

controlling the business

Be very clear about your position. You have no rulebook in a high-growth business; you only have constant change as a companion. The most valuable advice we can offer you is to heed the cash-flow points, undertake to constantly learn and never stop, plan professionally and review very regularly, and keep your feet on the ground. Keep the overheads sensible, resist the luxury cars and, above all, continue to lead the company, even when you have successfully developed a management team which is both capable and competent.

Good luck to you, for your journey is the most exciting of any entrepreneur, and is the one which holds the maximum risks as well as the maximum rewards.

PRACTICAL STEPS

- Positive cash flow is the most important element of your business.
- Collect your debts on time and negotiate longer terms with your suppliers.
- Keep stock to a minimum by effective supply chain management.
- Control your overheads by regular review.
- Be creative with remuneration packages. Cash is not the only motivator.
- Increase your credit lines to allow more flexible growth.
- Manage your banking relationship as you would a supplier.
- Leverage your balance sheet for correct gearing.
- Appoint the best people for the job.
- Have regard for the gross margin and breakeven points.
- Plan regularly to stay in control.
- Understand your business in the context of the marketplace.

supporting the business

legal and accounting

The appointment of lawyers or solicitors

The appointment of accountants and auditors

In your business, there are two key functions that will need to be addressed in the first few months of trading, if not before you start to trade. This is the search and selection of solicitors and accountants to your business. We will devote this chapter to these decisions, and give you some key pointers to a successful relationship and also how to manage your expectations.

THE APPOINTMENT OF LAWYERS OR SOLICITORS

For most small businesses, this appointment is usually based upon some previous contact with a solicitor, usually to the conveyancing work performed at the last house move. Cost is usually a major factor in this discussion, and the range of work that is needed is usually limited to the initial setting up of the legal entity from which you will trade. (See Chapter 1 for your shareholders' agreement content.)

This appointment, however, can have a marked effect upon your business from the point of view of external perception as well as operation matters and a successful outcome.

Before you make this particular decision, it is necessary for you to assess the likely range of services that you will call upon as your business grows and develops.

The following list is relevant to a small growing business, but is by no means exhaustive:

■ shareholders' agreements
■ forming of the legal entity
■ conveyancing of the purchase of the building or the lease contract
■ construction of your legal terms and conditions of trading
■ contracts of employment and directors' service contracts
■ assessment of the complex contracts that you may receive from a customer
■ various forms of debt collection
■ commentary on the various financial measures that you may wish to take over time

- the introduction of a new shareholder, or the separating of the ways of the existing ones
- defence against legal proceedings brought against your business
- dealing with the legal dismissal of employees
- contracting for specific sales or purchases of significance
- changes to the Memorandum and Articles of Association
- taking legal action against others for contractual failures
- reforming the business into a group or subsidiary as the business grows
- preparing legal audits for the purpose of additional finance, year 2000 issues, European Monetary Union issues, etc.
- preparing for the sale of the shares of the company in either a merger or disposal situation (see Chapter 10: 'The point of disposal or acquisition')
- addressing some of the higher-level tax limitation questions that you will face along the way.

Having recently started out in business, or taking your initial steps towards it, the above list may at first seem far removed from your ideas about the use of a solicitor, or indeed the subjects listed. Let us assure you that if your business continues to thrive and grow, you will almost certainly be covering 90 per cent of the items on the above list in the due course of time.

So now it will have become obvious to you that a general conveyancing solicitor will not necessarily be the best equipped to deal with your growing business. By using the Business Link in your area, coupled with the *Yellow Pages*, for instance, you will be able to draw up a shortlist of suitable solicitors. The next stage is to ask them for their corporate brochure, to give you a better feel for their service. Most solicitors will give you a free half-hour meeting which we recommend that you use in order to interview them and decide if you will be able to talk to them as business advisors in the future.

Don't be blinded by science, and don't be made to feel inadequate. Ask them for examples of their work, length of time in business, details of other clients in similar market sectors to you, and ask them to tell you what is their specialist area in their own opinion.

You will come out of this meeting with a feeling as to the level of interest that the solicitor showed you and your business. You will understand the level of expertise and experience in your size and sector and, above all, the feeling of whether you can work with this firm or individual in the future.

supporting the business

When you make your appointment, write to the solicitors concerned and tell them that you will be using their services, as and when, in your business. They, in turn, will add you to their client records and continue to send you information sheets about various events and services over the coming months and years.

When you deal with a solicitor, we must stress the following points.

The law as it stands is extremely unstructured, and outcomes are unpredictable.

We once sold a piece of equipment to a customer who shipped it to Belgium to his customer. The machine was used to print over 300 000 copies in two weeks, and then it broke down. Although it was sold with no warranty past the point of 'working upon receipt', and 300 000 copies represented 6 months' load normally, the customer refused to pay for the goods, and returned them broken. Our solicitor agreed that this was legally wrong, that we had a 100 per cent watertight case, and that we should sue the customer forthwith. The case took 6 months to get to court, and cost us over £2500 in legal fees, at which point the solicitor told us that, due to a technicality, our case had moved to a 50/50 position, and did we wish to proceed? If we did proceed, it would cost us a further £2000 in legal fees to our own solicitor. If we won, we would have recovered the £5000 owed to us but only half our legal costs. If we lost the case, we would have been liable for the customer's legal costs as well, estimated at £3500.

What would you have done? Was the solicitor negligent in his approach or advice?

Needless to say, we were very annoyed at the change in mood at the last minute, and we could add to this recollection many times during our business lives. It transpired that the solicitor was not negligent in any way and so the decision became a purely mathematical one based on probability. What did we do? We withdrew from the action, and negotiated a 'no costs' claim with our customer. We paid our £2500 solicitor's invoice, wrote off the £5000 debt, and retired to lick our wounds.

You never meet a poor solicitor.

They are in business to advise on the fickle points of the law and, regardless of the outcome, will seek to help you steer a path through the maze of complex procedures that will confront you when you press that legal button. They offer no guarantees, and the position will change with respect to your chances of success as the case proceeds. Whatever the outcome, you will end up paying your solicitor.

The personality of your appointed solicitor is, in our opinion, of great importance. We preferred to use a relatively aggressive solicitor, who would invoke various devices in law to push things along quickly. There is a balance between this and a gung-ho individual who is happy to play power games whilst billing you regularly.

There is always a temptation in business to trust a solicitor implicitly, and the usual rule of sending a purchase order to cover the work is often forgotten. This is due, in part, to the vague reflection on the final costs presented by the solicitor when you ask him the famous question 'How much will this cost?'

Our advice is simple.

- **Always send a written instruction** to your solicitor which spells out the details and background to the case. This document is vital to you in the future if you contend an invoice, or suggest that you have not been represented properly in court.
- **Always put a figure of financial authority** in this instruction so that, when it is exceeded, it will force the solicitor to ask for further written authorization. By adopting this method, you will always be in control of your costs, and will always have a rational approach to what is often an emotive issue.

If possible, and this is becoming more commonplace, link the payment of invoice to the outcome of the case. This is called contingency payment, and is finding its way over from America into our legal systems. At present, the range of actions that this applies to is restricted to personal damage claims, but there is a strong possibility that this will move to commercial litigation within a short time.

The basis for legal redress

In many small and growing businesses, there is often scant regard for the contractual basis for the relationship between customers and suppliers yet, without this framework, there is little basis for legal recourse if things go wrong.

We are, of course, talking about the terms and conditions of sale or purchase, and the associated contracts that accompany them. The informality of a

215

small business and the lack of control paperwork make this area of operations a time-consuming and unexciting one. Many business owners simply copy customers' terms onto their own letterhead, or simply use a few lines at the bottom of the purchase order to effect the terms of the business.

If you want to minimize your risk to the following:

- delayed payments of your debts
- return of goods for no reason
- increase in prices from your supplier between the order and delivery date
- retention of your goods despite not paying for them
- warranty claims and claims for damages, even though it is not your fault
- damaging delays in approval of the product or service
- inability to deliver to a site
- cancellation of the order even though you have already bought the materials …

… you must have a formalized set of terms and conditions drawn up that is relevant to your marketplace.

> **Tip:** If you are purchasing a piece of capital equipment such as a telephone switch or a computer system, it is worth discussing a separate purchase contract for this event. Don't use a standard purchase order.

There are two legal terms that you should understand, which will put into context our advice to you in the above section.

> **You must have formalized terms and conditions.**

These are simply *express terms* and *implied terms*. They are self-explanatory in their title.

The express terms in a contract, be it a verbal order, written purchase order or complicated contract, are the terms that are spelt out in no uncertain words. These are the terms such as payment, delivery, and the usual obvious variables, but they can also include the performance of the product or service, and the consequence of non-performance within a timescale. If these terms are expressed and are unambiguous, the chances of enforcing these clauses are relatively high.

The implied terms, as the name suggests, are those things that are common-sense and should always be the case, or are covered under other acts or legal statutes such as the consumer guarantees and rights, and the 'fit for purpose' type legislation. Even though the contract may not specifically mention them, there are implied terms relevant to all transactions.

The value of mediation and negotiation

Of course, you know the value of a negotiated outcome. It is cheaper, less fraught and usually ends up with both parties agreeing a basis for future business. It ends up being a more beneficial experience than the litigious route described above.

It can often be prudent to appoint a mediator in these circumstances, and give authority limits to this individual. Consultants will offer this service, as they are independent and business-focused. If both parties agree to this action, the consultant can be paid equally by both parties, and there is no allegiance to any single party, only to the outcome. Other situations will call for an independent professional body which is relevant to the industry that you are a part of. For instance, financial disputes can be referred to the Institute of Chartered Accountants as a body of authority.

It may well be that your contracts can stipulate the mediation clause as a precursor to any legal action, which may be a benefit to you as a business. Always look for a negotiated settlement, as often there is no clearcut right and wrong situation, no matter how strong you think your case is.

What to do when there is nowhere else to go

We can only stress that our own experiences make the course of litigation the one of last resort, as it can be the most expensive as well as the most unpredictable. The only winners are the legal representatives in every case.

If you are forced to go legal, make absolutely sure that you have completed the following list of actions:

■ Terms and conditions of the deal are clear, agreed and in force at the time of the deal.

■ The purchase order and all of the support documentation is in place and readily to hand.

■ Nothing was agreed verbally without having been put in writing.

- You are convinced that you cannot resolve this dispute by any other means.

- The financial risks have been quantified and written down.

- You have appointed a knowledgeable solicitor who understands your business.

- Your instructions to this solicitor are in writing with specific spend authority

- The overall cost structure and the chances of recovery are agreed along with the anticipated timescale for action. (Measure the solicitor by this written-down plan when you review the case periodically.)

- Your solicitor is matched against the company or person against whom you are taking action. If this is a London or large City-based firm, your solicitor cannot be a small, one-office provincial firm.

Summary

Remember that your solicitor works for you! Just because the details may appear to be complex, it does not preclude you from demanding a straight-forward answer to your questions.

Remember your solicitor works for you! The experiences that we have had in our business life, to date, have led us to understand that the law is extremely fickle and unpredictable. The appointment of legal representation of a high calibre can make a difference on occasions, but the value of mediation and negotiation cannot be stressed enough. If you have to press the legal buttons, do it once and do it hard.

Do not compromise your actions if this is the course that you are pursuing, and fight as though this is the last fight. Do not leave it to the solicitors, but use other pressures in the marketplace to push forwards. In the example of our court action mentioned above, we settled the legal case, but continued to lodge our complaints about the unprofessional behaviour of this customer with the international regulatory body to which most of our industry dealers subscribed.

Our last piece of advice is to ensure that your terms and conditions of trade are well structured, relevant and reviewed at least annually for the benefit of your business.

To help you to reduce your costs, particularly in the early years, we have included a directors' service contract and an employment contract on the attached diskette. [■ **Director's Contract.doc**, and **Contract.doc**]

THE APPOINTMENT OF ACCOUNTANTS AND AUDITORS

You will probably consider this one of the first things that you do after opening the bank accounts, and if you have been in business a while, will almost certainly have made the appointment already.

There is a legal requirement to keep accurate accounting records for your business and submit tax accounts on an annual basis. The submitted accounts are used in a variety of ways by various bodies, and here are just a few examples:

- *Companies House* requirements in the case of limited companies
- *Inland revenue* assessments
- *VAT* records for payments and reclaims
- credit assessment by *suppliers*
- insurance assessment by *insurance companies*
- interpretation by *customers* in light of awarding contracts
- used by *shareholders* in the review of the business
- used internally by *the board* to assess performance
- used by *potential purchaser* of the business to ascertain trading levels
- used by *your competition* to combat you in the marketplace

As you can see, there is a confusion of uses by various people who, in principle, have a polarity of needs. For the taxman, your profits should be kept low, but for the supplier, he needs to see you profitable. The board likewise, as well as the insurance companies, but the customer may like to see just average profit, whilst the shareholders may wish to distribute the profit prior to finalizing the net profit for the business.

The rules for preparing the accounts of the business are laid down by the accounting standards' body in the UK. Within this structure, there are specific rules relating to how profit is calculated, the various treatments of purchases and assets, and the taxation allowances as laid down by the government of the day. Within the documents, however, there is certain scope for movement.

For example, your business may decide to buy an asset valued at, say, £10 000. If the asset is useful in its present form for a number of years, you may decide to apply a depreciation policy of 7 years' straight line. The tax treatment is to allow 15 per cent of the reducing value as a tax allowance, which is another option for the depreciation policy. In the first method, your business will write off £1428.57 against the annual profits each and every year for seven years, and in the second method, a total of £1500 in the first year, £1275 in the second, £1083.75 in the third, and so on. You can easily see the difference in the impact on the net profits of the business over time.

What we have illustrated rather simply here is that the rules of accounting are open to some degree of interpretation, as long as the policies adopted by your business are both legal and consistent. This possibility must be reflected in the shareholders' agreement as to the treatment of profit. If you are just starting out in business, or have been trading for a while, but in start-up mode, your profits may not be high enough for you to be overly concerned at this stage. We invite you to look ahead when you make the selection of the accountants to your business, and ask yourself how hard they will work on your behalf to maximize your position at all times.

> The rules of accounting are open to interpretation.

The accountant will need to be of a size and qualification as to offer your business the appropriate audit service when you have grown to a greater size or when you operate as an incorporated business.

The difference between accounts and audit is straightforward. The preparation of the accounts for taxation purposes is mandatory for all business bodies. The process of audit is to validate or test the representation of these accounts in the context of the business. It can be likened to the school class exam report, where the teacher marks the work, and the headmaster makes the appropriate comment at the end of term!

When you select your accountant, which must be a reselection process each and every year, you must identify the following points as a starting point.

- Does your accountant have full audit capability if you believe that you will require it?
- Does the practice have a resident tax specialist and VAT specialist if appropriate?
- Is the firm of accountants of a similar or larger size than your own business?
- Who will read your accounts?
- Do you propose selling your business within, say, 3 years?
- Do you conduct overseas business and use the various tax, duty and currency schemes available?
- Is the personality of the accountant of a sufficiently proactive nature to continually provide support to your business?
- Does your accountant understand computerized accounts?

These are just some of the questions that you may like to consider.

The accountant can have a remarkable effect upon a business and its ability to grow. We have seen many instances of the accountant offering staid, or even incorrect advice to small businesses, which has really held them back from growing, or even being profitable. When these businesses have changed accountants, the effect has been so dramatically positive, with cash-flow improvement, profit improvement and reduced taxation bills that the business has been able to go on and really prosper the way it should have done in earlier years.

The preparation of your accounts

Once you have read the Chapter 4: 'Training to stay alive' – Finance module, you will be well prepared to go on and assess the stages of the accountant in preparing your accounts, and examine some of the issues for which you must be prepared. The training module is a precursor to this section, so if you haven't done so already, refer to Chapter 4 right now!

■ Accounting policies

If you have traded for a year or more, it is likely that your accountant, with or without your knowledge, has adopted accounting policies for your business. It is vital that you understand these without delay, and identify whether they comply with your needs in regard of your shareholders' agreement and your needs with respect to profit levels.

> **Your end-of-year date can be very important.**

The accounting policies will refer to depreciation, treatment of fixed assets and capitalization limits, etc. Do not confuse these with the accounting standards, which are laid down in law.

■ Tax year-end

Your end-of-year date can be very important, and should be chosen with care. It has a direct effect upon the tax treatment of your accounts, and must be understood and changed if necessary. Instruct your accountant to tell you the reason for your end-of-year date with reference to taxation charges.

■ Sales cut-off

An important discipline in the formation of your accounting practices is the cut-off point. The date by which you physically deliver the goods or service to the customer must not be any later than the date by which you invoice the customer for these items. Forward invoicing is not allowable under accounting rules, and should not be undertaken in the preparation of accounts for release to external bodies.

■ Treatment of assets

The inclusion of smaller items of hardware and, indeed, software into the fixed asset register, with a considered write-down policy, can have a marked difference on the profits of the business. If you choose to incorporate just about everything, your profit level will increase.

■ VAT and PAYE treatment

If you are a net exporter of goods or services, you are likely to be in a VAT reclaiming position each quarter. If you contact the VAT office, and explain that you are a small business in a net reclaim position, you can negotiate a monthly VAT return. This means that you are able to receive the VAT refund earlier and improve your cash-flow.

Keep accurate stock records.

Conversely, if you employ yourself and/or staff in your business, and, as such, are liable to collect the PAYE tax every month, it is possible, where this amount is small, to arrange to pay this money over to the inland revenue on a quarterly basis. This not only saves time, but also improves your cash-flow.

■ Stock

The last major sensitive area in your business accounting process is the stock that you hold. It is vital that you keep accurate stock records and also try to analyze the stock movement by line item by again keeping records. The value of this exercise will come clear in the preparation of your accounts. Part of the accountant's role is to judge whether the stock that you hold is valued correctly for the market conditions, and whether the value that you have attributed to each line item is the lower of the stock value, or the net realizable value in the marketplace.

In the event that good records are not kept, the accountant and auditor will err on the side of prudence and propose stock devaluations in order to protect the balance sheet position. The devaluations are made against the profit and loss account, and so reduce the profits of the business. Whereas this can be a useful device in itself, without good records, it is not one that you are in control of.

In a fast-growth business, it is imperative that the balance sheet remains strong, and uncontrolled stock write-downs are a source of annoyance.

■ Other financing issues

Your accountant must be able to help you with other aspects of your business relating to the positive cash-flow of the business. Such questions as 'Should I look at invoice discounting or factoring?' should be an area where expert advice is at hand. Other problems such as, for instance, preparing the cash-flow statements for the purpose of securing greater credit lines with the bank or other sources of finance should also be something that your accountant can help you with.

Summary

We have now examined some of the areas that you will need to consider in the appointment of your accountant, and some of the questions that you must ask to qualify the expertise of the firm that you are considering.

We appointed one of the 'big six' accountants when we were just 4 years into our business, because of our stated intention to sell the business in a 5-year time period. The markets would then see a large and reputable auditor preparing our accounts; therefore proving our net worth and profit streams became a little easier. We also sent out a message to customers, supplier and banks alike, as to our professional intentions with respect to our business. If we had wanted to continue trading for a longer period of time, we would have taken slightly different decisions and probably appointed a middle-ground accountant who would have charged us less, and would have taken more interest in the development of our business.

> The appointment of professional support bodies is of great importance in business development.

When you reappoint each year, ensure that the formal written quotation is submitted for the following year's audit and preparation, and don't forget that the tax computations are usually invoiced separately. Be specific about what you want. The audit and accounts submission is only a small part of the value that a good accountant can add to your business and, if in doubt about this, ask the question.

supporting the business

Summary of chapter

The appointment of either of these professional support bodies is of great importance in your business development. The messages that you send to the stakeholders in your business will be powerful ones, and the quality of support that you will gain from the right appointments will be worth every penny.

Remember the solicitor and the accountant all work for you. Make sure that you instruct them clearly, measure the performance and contain the costs to a stated figure. Above all, don't be afraid to put the service out to tender each year. In the cycle of development of your business, you may just find that the support needs will change and that an alternative provider will give you the edge in the market.

PRACTICAL STEPS

- Appoint solicitors and accountants as you would suppliers.

- Consider the style of your business in the future when you appoint.

- Instruct in writing with a monetary maximum at all times, for everything.

- Ensure you devise and then review periodically a proper set of terms and conditions.

- Don't be afraid to change if the service fails to meet your needs.

- Don't allow yourself to be baffled by complex words. If the accountant or solicitor is good enough, they can always explain in plain English.

the point of disposal or acquisition

Disposal

Acquisitions

For many businesses, the point in time when you may have the opportunity to sell your company may seem a very long way away. Indeed, you might have plans in place to continue your business until retirement or some other such milestone in your life.

The decision to sell your business may, in fact, be forced upon you by the movement in the marketplace, or the low performance of your sales, for example. On the flip-side of the coin, the opportunity to purchase another business, either in part or in whole, may leverage opportunities that you have yet to consider in your business plans.

This chapter looks at the hands-on advice that we can offer in conjunction with a good accountant and an even better solicitor. More deals of this nature fail to deliver the expected outcome than succeed, which is a shocking statistic. The point at which you decide to acquire or dispose of a business is one of incredible emotion and vulnerability.

You probably read in the paper or on CeeFax of the huge sums of money that are paid for household name businesses on the Stock Exchange. The small business league is no different in principle, but the understanding and resources available to manage these complex events are often lacking.

We will attempt to offer you some first-hand advice as to how to minimize your risks and increase your chances of success in what is generally considered a lottery draw of an outcome.

DISPOSAL

For many of us, the opportunity to sell our growing business for a large capital sum is an overwhelmingly juicy idea. All those noughts and happy retirement possibilities come crowding into our minds as the prospect of a stress-free time looms on the sun-setting horizon.

Unfortunately reality is somewhat removed from this ideal. The reality is that two-thirds of all company sales do not integrate into the new environment, and end up failing. The consequence for many business owners is that the sums of money are never in fact paid, as the contract of sale allows circumstances to be accounted for that will reduce the sums owed.

There are probably two basic scenarios, but many permutations of the reasons why you, as a business owner, will end up discussing a sale of your company.

■ The first is an approach by another, probably bigger company, who wishes to purchase your company for the marketplace you are in, the customer base that you have developed or the profit streams and cash that your business may generate. If you receive an approach, your bargaining power is greatly enhanced and your chances of success in exiting from your business are that much higher as long as you follow the basic rules that we have offered below.

■ The second reason is that your business, for whatever reason, is struggling to make things work. The marketplace may have changed, the staff may not be right for the business, you may have exhausted your options, or, indeed, the cash-flow may be wrong for the continued development of the business. As we said earlier, there are many different combinations of the above, but the essence is that you are looking to find a suitor for exit purposes.

> **If you receive an approach, your bargaining power is greatly enhanced**

For the rest of this chapter we will concentrate on the second scenario. Once this is understood it will be easy to map this advice onto the first illustration.

When you have made the decision to dispose of your company, it is very important for you to document a Head of Agreement that all shareholders can sign. This document will simply seek to list the various actions and review points that will take place, and should be amended from time to time to take account of the increase in information or numbers, for instance. This document can act as an audit trail if any single shareholder should claim misinformation or lack of understanding at any time. If you hold regular shareholder meetings, formalize them, minute them and attach any supplementary information that has been discussed.

The order of play can be summarized as follows:

1 Draw up Head of Agreement between all shareholders.
2 Inform your accountant of choice, which may not be your retained accountant.
3 Inform the appointed solicitor who will act for you.

4 Be prepared to spend time at a senior level, in order to formulate a memorandum of sale document. This will describe your business in great detail and append accounting information and forward forecasts. The approximate cost of this document, usually prepared by the accountants or consultants, is around £4000–6000.

5 Decide who you will approach with an anonymous paragraph about your business in order to flush out interested parties. The most likely purchasers are to be found in your competitors, or suppliers, or a complementary partner who may wish to invest in your market and may not be there at present. If you do not have likely names to hand, the accountant or consultant that you have appointed will provide lists. Failing this, you may decide to advertise the business, again anonymously, in the *Financial Times*, for instance.

6 Ensure that you understand the process of confidentiality agreements, and don't approach a business that you do not feel comfortable with.

7 The timescale for this process will run for about 6 weeks on average.

8 At the end of this time, you will have issued the sale memorandum to many companies under strict confidentiality terms. The process will ask for all offers to be received by a set date.

9 At this time, hopefully, you will have three or so interested offers for your business, none of which will be the price that you would like!

10 The process of direct meetings can now take place in order to ascertain the potential match between the two businesses. Various discussions can take place about the structure of a deal, the amounts payable, the timescales, etc.

11 If you can agree a deal, the legal process can start to roll, and usually takes around 3 months to complete.

There may be some variation to the above running order, depending upon the type of business that you have to sell, but, on average, the points listed above will give you a clear idea of what to expect. This should be made clear to all shareholders before you start this action, and agreements must be obtained from all parties, indicating a minimum selling price if this is relevant.

The first order of business, then, is to appoint a firm or an individual to represent you in the process of sale. This is clearly a vital decision, one that you must take steadily, and after having met and interviewed three or four possible candidates.

Your options are as follows:

- a firm of accountants – either known to you by appointment, or selected for the task
- a firm of solicitors, some of whom specialize in this area
- a disposal specialist firm, usually found through either your accountant, your local Chamber of Commerce, the Institute of Directors, or business directories
- an individual consultant who may specialize in your market.

There may be certain advantages to one of the above in your own business, but it is worth selecting one from each category and having a meeting with them. Ask them how they would approach the sale, and compare the response to the above checklist. Discuss the number of deals that they perform on a monthly basis, and ask for three references.

Don't be hesitant in contacting these refererees, as the information given to you may well influence the appointment in what is the most critical decision of your business life to date. Then make sure that you speak to the person who will actually sell your business with you, and ask him how pleased he/she is to represent you in the marketplace.

> **Tip:** *Don't select a representative who does not demonstrate competence in your market sector, or who usually deals with businesses who are different in size to your own.*

The first tangible evidence of sale is the production of the sale memorandum, which is usually put together by the accountant or consultant. The way in which this is written will have a direct bearing upon your success in achieving a successful sale. Remember that this is your ultimate sales proposal – you only have one go at this!

> **Tip:** *Don't let the sales memorandum degenerate into a boring accountant's document.*

Ensure that the production of this document has your first-hand input, and don't be frightened to change it to satisfy yourself. This is the first representation of your business that a potential purchaser will see. They have to get

supporting the business

excited about it, and be interested in your story of growth and marketplace sales. They have to want to buy you! There are certain bits that will need to be completely factual and unambiguous, and there are other sections, such as the executive summary, where an opportunity exists to motivate the reader in a positive way.

In the sale process of our own business, we appointed a mergers and acquisitions consultant to work alongside us at specific stages of the deal. This was useful in so far as our experiences of selling a business were zero, and the appraisal of various issues was of some benefit, particularly in the negotiating stages.

Managing the business through the sales cycle

From the moment that you appoint selling representation, and instruct the preparation of a sales memorandum, your business enters a time of greater vulnerability than ever before.

If you have staff, you will need to decide whether you tell them or not. If you do, they may leave. If you don't, they will surely find out at some stage and rumours are very destructive. If you are selling the business to strengthen the future, you may be able to tell a convincing story, which will keep them motivated.

If the business has been through difficult times, it would be a natural reaction, both for you as well as your staff, to focus upon the point in 3 to 5 months' time when everything will be happily resolved.

More quality businesses go into liquidation trying to effect a sale than at any other time. You must manage your business even more carefully and even more vigilantly in order to survive this period of high risk.

It will be a difficult task managing your staff during this time, as the news will undoubtedly leak into the marketplace. Think carefully about your response to the questions from customers and suppliers that will inevitably come in the short term. Your credit rating may suffer at this point, as your suppliers will recognize the increase risks to your business, and seek to reduce their exposure accordingly.

Valuation of your business

At the point of preparing your sales document, there will come a time when the famous question that you have been dying to ask gets answered: 'How much is the business worth?'

> **'How much is the business worth?'**

Here are some of the factors that will be considered when the valuation is performed.

- How long have you been in business?
- What marketplace do you sell into?
- Are you in control of your marketplace?
- Do you sell something that is unique or do you add value in a unique way?
- Does your business attract 'quality earnings'? These may be long-term customer contracts, royalties, leasing commissions, licence fees to the customer base, guaranteed earnings of other sorts.
- Who are your customers, and are these customers desirable (blue chip, for instance)?
- What level of sales do you have?
- What is the underlying profitability?
- What is your net asset position?
- Do you have an attractive future in an expanding market?
- Are you people based, or product based for success?
- Does your business rely upon you as a person in order to be successful, or do you have a strong management team that runs the daily business?

There are probably many others, but you will now see the major factors that will underpin and enhance your company's value.

There is one other term that you need to understand in the pricing of a business, and that is *'price earnings multiple'*.

If you take your average net profits, assuming that they are relatively consistent over the last few years, and deduct tax at the appropriate rate, you will end up with a net after tax figure. The price earnings multiple (PEM or PE ratio) is a number between 1 and, say, 30, which the marketplace will support as your value. If you look in the *Financial Times*, the right-hand column will tell you what the PE is for each company listed.

In the engineering sector, for example, a factor on average of 17 is expected, whereas the biotech sector, which is generally thought to be very high growth, can carry a PE of anything from 20 to 50. These figures are for public quoted companies of a certain size and position in the market.

We now bring you down to earth with a bump, and tell you that, for a small private business in an average sector, with a few years' trading and average profits, the PEM is usually around 4–9.

The final figure is an assessment of the various factors listed above, and you can self-score on this basis.

ILLUSTRATION

A light engineering consultancy, employing 15 people, with turnover of £750 000 to 20 or so blue chip companies, producing a profit of about £70 000 each year. The market is static, and there is no formal management team in place. The business has forward contracts of 3 months' worth of work, and relies upon the staff employed to maintain the relationships with the clients. The business has been trading at this level for about 4 years, and has a net asset position of £250 000. The business is considered to be competent and leading the way in solution provision to engineering problems.

The position of purchaser will be to appraise the business as follows:

- management is weak, but is not too much of a problem as long as the staff stay in place and the customers transfer
- the 20 customers are a good spread
- the customers are blue chip and can probably be developed for greater return
- forward contracts are OK, but what happens then?
- the engineering sector is not in great shape right now, so there is a risk of revenue reduction in the coming year
- the £70 000 profit is OK by percentage, and there is a case that as a purchaser I could retain more to the bottom line by using my business methods

As a purchaser, we would be hesitant in light of the current sector performance. It may well be, however, that we have a business that would benefit from this acquisition and would price it therefore as follows.

Assuming little fixed assets and stock to complicate the net asset position, we would pay pound for pound in cash the £250 000, assuming that the business could prove the recovery of the debtors was assured. The profit streams seem rather more tenuous, however, and we would find a way to defer any more payment until we had proven the transfer of the business was successful. The profits of £70 000, which equate to just over £50 000 after a nominal tax rate, would then attract a PEM of, say, around 5 as a starter for negotiation. The payment of this, however, would, as we said above, be deferred using a suitable earn-out instrument.

The total indicative offer that we would put forward would be £500 000, with half paid in cash, the other half paid in deferred cash or shares.

We hope that this illustration shows how a deal is priced, and how the valuation is arrived at. It must be understood that this is not a precise science, and that one person's valuation may differ widely from another.

When your business is valued, ensure you ask how the figure is arrived at, and get it put in writing.

> *Don't accept professionals' advice without understanding and don't be afraid to ask; if you are or if the answers are not satisfactory, change advisors.*

Earn-out contracts

For many small businesses, as we have just illustrated above, it may not be possible to sell your business for a satisfactory amount unless you agree to a form of earn-out. This, in essence, means that part, or in some cases all of the consideration is paid as a result of a series of equations or conditions being met, which means the business is successfully working within the purchaser's own market. The earn-out contract is usually based upon a net profit calculation over one-quarter to 5 years, say.

If you can avoid an earn-out agreement, do so.

However, for many owners this is the only way of effecting a sale of the business, and therefore they are a very common mechanism for the sale of small businesses. You may be faced with this option at some time, and we have prepared some key tips for you to heed when considering an earn-out value of your company.

Our words of caution stem from meeting many entrepreneurs who have lost huge sums of money by agreeing to inappropriate earn-out contracts.

supporting the business

233

1 Ensure that you get as much cash up front as possible, as if things go wrong, you may have difficulty proving earn-out contracts in a legal court due to interpretable events.

2 Remember that you will not have control once you have sold the business.

3 Make sure the definition of net profit is very clearly defined. Ensure that the effect of year 2000 and EMU are carefully handled within the context of net profit calculations.

4 Stipulate the amount of control that you will have over your 'old business' in the context of this arrangement.

5 Make sure that you list the 'will not do to the business' actions that could have a detrimental effect upon the profits.

6 Make sure the cultures fit, as this is the most common form of failure to integrate.

7 Remember that the deferred consideration may not be paid at all.

8 Be extremely careful about signing warranties that give a right of clawback to the purchaser.

Agreeing the deal

We return to our sales scenario, having prepared our sales memorandum, valued the business, and marketed to a defined marketplace. Our input to the document has proved good, as we now find that, in the defined timescale, we have three responses showing an indicative offer for the business. All three are on the low side, but this is normally the case at this stage.

Along with your advisor, you can now convene meetings with the three parties in order to persuade them to increase their offers, based upon the positive experience of meeting with yourself, and possibly a tour of the business.

This is inevitably a time of great excitement for you and, in the majority of cases, one of great relief. If the numbers look all right, and you have managed to negotiate an amount of cash up-front to the earn-out contract, you may be looking forward to the great day with blind anticipation.

There are two major issues that we now urge you to identify. The first is the cultural fit, and the second concerns warranties and indemnities.

Cultural fit

The biggest single cause of failure to integrate within a purchaser's business, and therefore failure of earn-out, is the differing cultures within two businesses. If you have grown your business over a number of years, and have a core of loyal workers, it is likely that they, and you, will be comfortable about the way things are done. Indeed, the unspoken values, the way that you react and address the needs of your employees may form the bond of trust that pre-empts any contract of employment.

By exposing the business, through sale, to another's way of doing things, perhaps not as caring as your own, the risk of employees becoming uncomfortable and disillusioned increases dramatically.

This problem can be foreseen in every single sale or purchase of a business, and at the public listed company end, there are SWAT teams ready to move into the acquired business in order to smooth the transitions, ensuring maximum performance with minimal loss of staff. Change management accounts for about 23 per cent of the worldwide consultancy market, and post-acquisition is a significant portion of this multimillion dollar marketplace. We will concentrate upon post-acquisition planning later in this section, but we would now like to return to the basic cultural issues.

It is vital that you spend enough time in the prospective purchaser's business prior to agreeing a sale, in order to identify any major cultural issues that will cause problems.

Listen to your instincts and don't paper over the cracks.

It is far better to address these concerns *now*, before you have signed over control of your business. Identify any concerns and make sure that you are satisfied that they have been addressed. If there is any inkling of a cultural mismatch, assume the worst, and either withdraw or get paid entirely in cash.

Understand that the business is unlikely to survive if the culture is not within a similar band to your own, as employees quickly leave and the essence of your business will be lost. This will affect your payments receivable for the business, if, indeed, the business survives this tumultuous time at all.

supporting the business

Due diligence

When you have agreed in principle the various terms of sale, there will then begin a process initiated by the purchaser called due diligence. This usually requires their accountants to have uninterrupted access to your business and all of its historic records, for the purpose of finding anything unusual that might cause problems later. The visit lasts a number of days, and will require a large percentage of your time to be spent finding documents such as insurance policies, leases, employment contracts, tax returns, accounts information galore, sales figures and analysis, as well as supplier information, etc.

> In every sale contract, there are warranties and indemnities.

The findings will become the subject of a detailed report to the purchaser, to give them certain assurances that things are as you say they are. If the documentation is less than strong in certain areas, this may be raised as an issue in a subsequent meeting. Unless your business is hiding a great secret, or your interpretation of events does not support the reality, then the due diligence process is usually a lengthy formality. You can compare it to an RAC check on a car before you hand over the cheque.

Warranties and indemnities

In every sale contract, there are clauses called warranties and indemnities, which you will undoubtedly be asked to agree to.

> *Tip: Sign as few of these clauses as possible, and indemnify nothing.*

The purchaser, on the other hand, will want you to offer guarantees about everything possible, and impose a financial penalty wherever possible.

The outcome is a position in the middle, but usually favouring the purchaser at the end of the day. The contract of sale is a document of shared risk, but you must be aware that you will share a greater portion of that risk if you enter into an earn-out contract. The odds will be stacked against you, and you must treat each 'harmless – won't ever happen' warranty statement as a cash claim in your own mind. Remember, if it won't ever happen, why is the clause in the contract in the first place?

Having got this far, don't be bullied or pushed into something you would not normally agree to in real life.

Planning

Having been through the processes of due diligence, and spent time with the purchaser prior to commitment, it will be possible to agree a formalized plan of management – *post* acquisition.

When a company is acquired, it goes through a marked change and organizational crisis. The trauma experienced by all employees stems from the fact that the acquisition represents a clear break from the past, and they therefore need reinstructing as to their future role. Indeed, you as an owner, if you continue to work in the business, will need a new mandate if you are to remain comfortable. Failure to reinstruct will leave managers traumatized, disorganized, disorientated and to the point of resignation for no good reason at all.

It is well documented that most businesses will lose profits in the first 3 to 6 months after being acquired, and this is the major cause of the problem. If you have an earn-out to make, you can ill afford this period of lower profits, and so we advise you to forward plan in order to alleviate the difficulties.

When you devise your plan, take into account the fact that most people will expect changes in the first few months. Indeed, if changes don't happen, you may find the same disruptive symptoms, as the perception will be that the purchaser is not interested in them! The human element to this plan is the most significant. All acquisitions start with the accounting systems, and then pause to find direction. Your plan must start with the people, and then keep going with the people, and not stop.

> **Your plan must start with the people.**

In our experience more goodwill is lost in the first 2 months by inaction than by anything else.

The plan that you propose must be all-encompassing, and well documented to the best detail that you can deliver in the timescales. It must, of course, take account of the earn-out conditions that have been agreed, and this may be a good time to agree certain allowances for certain actions that you would like to happen, but cannot allow to happen if the profit calculation prevents this from being sensible. In the face of a good plan, the purchaser should welcome this dialogue, and it will also focus a little more clearly on any cultural difficulties.

supporting the business

General issues

Your professional advisors should highlight the obvious issues such as tax clearances and planning, and so we will simply list them here. Indeed, individual needs are so varied that this is the most that we can provide in this section.

Before we move on to a 'hot tips' list for disposal of your business, please do not forget the most important thing in the whole process ...

> *Don't forget to look after your business during this time ... the deal may fail, but your business must go on.*

TIPS FOR DISPOSAL OF YOUR BUSINESS

1 Choose your advisors carefully. Ensure synergy and understanding.

2 Plan your tax position as early as possible.

3 Don't forget to look after the business ... the deal may fail.

4 If you don't understand anything, stop until you do.

5 Gain a written shareholders' agreement.

6 Minute all shareholder meetings on a monthly and event basis.

7 Interview at least three representatives who could sell your business.

8 Ensure you input positive statements to the sale memorandum.

9 Manage the sale process internally for minimum disruption to the business.

10 Prepare for external customer or supplier enquiries.

11 Get the valuation calculation in writing.

12 Audit the prospective purchasers for cultural fit.

13 Spend time within their business as part of your own due diligence.

14 Resist earn-out contracts.

15 Take as much cash up front as possible: cash talks – shares can walk.

16 Use an external negotiator if possible.

17 The year 2000 and EMU liabilities must be understood and defined.

18 Warrant as little as possible, treat each clause as a claim.

19 Post-disposal management plan must be in place before the legal contracts are fully drawn.

ACQUISITIONS

The process of acquiring a business has already been described in reverse terms above. Your business may have reached a plateau point in its development, or you may find a business or competitor that is struggling, and the terms may be right for you. If you are actively looking to acquire in order to fulfil a strategy in the marketplace, for example, the appointment of advisors are an identical discipline to that described above in the disposal section. Your accountant is able to offer a targeting service to find a match for your criteria, or you may choose to undertake this work yourself.

> **Target your company carefully.**

The advantage of doing some of the work yourself is that you are able to gain an enormous amount of market information that may be of great use to you as a business. Indeed, the information that you come across in pursuit of an acquisition can be almost as useful as the acquisition itself.

Remember what we said in the above section about a company approaching you with a need to buy your business, and how much stronger your hand is when this happens. Well, this time you are purchasing, and it is very important at the pre-approach stage to play things down, and not to show excitement to the prospective business.

Target your company carefully, and ensure that it portrays all of the elements that you are looking for. Do not compromise, as you are sure to be disappointed later.

> **Post-acquisition management planning is vital**

Remember that the cultural fit between two companies is one of the single most important factors that will make an acquisition successful, or cause you an expensive failure.

Planning

Post-acquisition management planning is vital if the integration of the purchased business is to be successful. A detailed planning session with the directors and management team of the business will enable you to get under the skin of the business before you buy it. It can be the most useful exercise that becomes more revealing than your due diligence process, as this is live action with the team of people that you are going to buy. If you can get

supporting the business

agreement to this activity, you might want to consider using an external and independent facilitator or consultant to help the session proceed smoothly.

Clearly, the purchasing of another business is a high risk, considering the large percentage of failures that result. You, as the buyer, will want to limit the cash-out in the first stage, and retain the support of the incumbent managing director in order to effect a successful handover. You will probably want to create an earn-out to protect your initial investment, but you should be aware of the pros and cons of this mechanism. They are listed in the above section under disposals, and so we will not repeat that list. From the purchaser's point of view, the earn-out can be a way of preventing you from fully integrating the new business, and will therefore delay the benefits of your purchase for the duration of the earn-out.

Points to remember

Be creative

Our advice to you is simple. If an earn-out is the only sensible mechanism for buying the business, be creative about the measurements of the earn-out, and don't just link it to the net profit created. Use the post-acquisition planning session to create a flexible understanding, which you may be able to translate into the purchase contract.

Liabilities

It is vital that you as a buyer know that the due diligence process has identified the potential liabilities of the acquired business with respect to the year 2000 and EMU currency risks. Make sure that your advisors are well briefed in these subjects and, if you are unsure, seek an independent view.

Service contracts

Be careful about the employee service contracts terms, which may include some liabilities that you may not identify. If employees served 20 years, the possibility of replacing them with the different skills that the merged business needs, or simply the rationalizing of common departments, will cost you a small fortune in redundancy payments or severance pay. Pay attention to the fringe benefits match between your business and the purchased business, as these can often cause discomfort between the two workforces.

Management strengths

The advantages and disadvantages of acquisitive growth will be particular to your own business. The single most important factor in the decision of whether to acquire or not is to question your strengths as a management team. Acquiring a business will be extremely time-consuming, and may require both you and other members of your team to be taken away from your core business for periods. If you get it right, the rewards can be forthcoming. Misjudge the situation, and the crisis that could result has been known to financially cripple the acquiring business.

Timing is everything in the acquisition stakes, for the cycle of your own business, and the stage of development of the acquired business.

effective use of technology

The telephone

Use of the personal computer

In this chapter we will be discussing the use and advantages of new technology. The various inventions that have found their way to the commercial market in such a short space of time will really give your business a competitive advantage if harnessed and embraced by you within your business.

We have come out of the Industrial Revolution at the turn of the century and have seen incredible advancements in all areas of our lives, leading to the invention of the first computer in 1948. The computer revolution has affected all our lives, whether we know it or not, and today there is very little that happens in our lives that has not been touched by the influence of the computer at some stage in its journey to our door.

> The big word these days is 'information'.

In the last 10 years we have seen quantum leaps in the ability to communicate, both in telephony, computer data and physical terms. We termed this period the communications revolution, which is a change process that we are still in the middle of today. The advancements in our ability to communicate have now led to an information glut, which has been the result of our quest for that elusive paperless office!

We would now like to explore some of the subjects and inventions that you can use today to help you to manage your business lives. Read this chapter, and then read Chapter 12: 'Time and stress management', to put into context the advantages of the effective use of IT.

The big word these days is 'information'. How do we get more information to turn into leads? How do we get it to our sales people when they are out on the road? How do we sift the information we need from the mountain of information we don't?

One of the answers lies in smart communications. We will now examine some of the options that will have an effect upon your efficiency in the short term. If you find an area that you wish to pursue, dedicate time with your local Business Link via their IT competence centres, or with a dedicated vendor, in order to understand the issues more clearly.

THE TELEPHONE

Of course you know how important the phone is! But how many of you really understand the power of the telephone switch. If you are a very small business, you may not have invested in a switch, but there are a large number of services available from your provider, be that BT or a cable company, that will allow you to reroute calls, accept messages and page you with the message. The use of mobile telephones needn't be expensive, and can be tailored to meet your needs.

If you are a little bigger as an organization, you may have leased or purchased a basic switchboard. By carefully selecting or upgrading periodically, you will be able to use the additional functions such as speed-dials, auto callback,

> **There are many advantages of using a PC as a telephone.**

caller ID, etc. If you need to buy a new telephone switchboard, as many businesses do in order to offer expansion to the number of lines or operator extensions, stop and consider an alternative.

The PC is replacing the telephone. Yes, the entire functionality of a telephone system can be mapped onto a PC for the same costs, and the results can be startling. The flexibility and additional functions can make an enormous difference in the way that you run the business.

For example, information automatically faxed upon request by a client, transfers to your mobile, as if it were an extension in the office; tracking of all calls made and received down to the extension; the use of what we call 'pop screens' which automatically strip off the call line identifier (which is the technical bit that allows us to dial 1471 and get the last number called) and then auto-seeks the sales database for the customer record. If found, the customer record interrupts your PC session at the same time as your telephone rings. If you transfer the call, the screen follows the call, and so your employees will have immediate and amazing access to the customer's details, which is something that your customer will quickly warm to.

There are many advantages of using a PC as a telephone, and they are too numerous to list here. A term to watch out for is a vendor who claims competence in CTI, which stands for 'computer telephony integration'. This technology is now affordable for the small business, and can offer you the look and feel of a business very much larger, which is good for business, good for the customer, and good for the bottom line.

supporting the business

245

USE OF THE PERSONAL COMPUTER

The Personal computer was born into businesses in about 1982 when IBM launched their first PC-XT. Since that time, we have seen the number of PCs in the world reach incredible proportions, and in business today, it is widely recognised as being of great value. For many small businesses, the need to buy a PC is sometimes a kneejerk reaction. The reasons for the machine become lost, as we mumble something about computerized accounts and greater efficiency.

We met a company who ran a fleet of vehicles a few years ago, in which the manager tracked the whereabouts of the 15 or so vans and motorbikes using a huge whiteboard. On this board he had the driver's name, customer details, estimated time of arrival, costs, route information, etc. A computer vendor had just left his office and the director was very excited about the possibility of a new computer system. The business didn't own a PC to date, and so they had no experience of use, yet the computer vendor was happy to sell this company four PCs, and no training.

It turned out that they had suggested replacing the whiteboard with an Excel spreadsheet, yet the customer didn't know why. He would have had to open a file, look at a 14" screen, scroll through the screens until he found the correct entry. Then he wouldn't have been able to see all of the information relating to the job without scrolling horizontally. The fact of the matter was, the customer needed his whiteboard, as to replace it would have degraded his ability to function.

PCs generally will save you time when the systems are correctly set up, but don't be lured into thinking that they will solve all problems within the business. State your business need for the PC, write it down and understand then how the PC will address the objectives. If it is not clear, don't buy one.

Having said all that, we are firmly of the opinion that, when used correctly, PCs will save you a huge amount of time, and more importantly will give you greater opportunities in the market. The use of word processing has revolutionized our small businesses by creating the opportunity for the small business to create some really great-looking documents that were previously the province of the larger firm.

Using Word or similar packages, you can now get instant spellcheckers, grammar checkers; a host of drawing tools, and presentation tools.

The Excel spreadsheet allows us to create complex scenario planning models, and to control our businesses in a way that would have taken five or more accounts clerks to perform the same function.

The PowerPoint or freelance graphics packages will allow your imagination to be freed, with the ability to create some very professional and exciting slide presentations, which can now be fully animated at the touch of a button, and projected onto the wall directly from your PC using a special projector.

Computerizing your accounting functions can be the first step in using the PC in your business. The advantages of using Sage, or equivalent package, can give you direct benefits. The annual accountant's fees could be reduced, as your computer has performed much of the checking and audit functions that would normally take manual clerks many days to complete.

The management accounts can be prepared quickly and so monthly reporting can take place. This is essential if your business is growing, or if you are experiencing difficulties and need to keep a special eye on the accounts position. If you embark upon this route as a first step, approach your accountant first, as they often have people who can install the software and train you as the user in the best practices of using computerized accounts (see the later sections in this chapter for training needs).

The PC fax user

If you already have a PC, you will also probably have a facsimile machine as an essential piece of equipment. If you receive a lot of faxes, you may wish to consider the use of the PC as a fax machine. Using Microsoft Outlook, or other specific fax software, you can attach a modem to the PC and have it answer the fax line as it rings.

The fax that would normally have printed out on the expensive and curly fax paper will now appear as a document within your PC. You can click on it and read as normal and, if you need to, you can print it to your normal A4 paper printer.

In our own business, our sales force used to send out around 200 faxes per night to prospective customers, who were, in fact, other dealers. It would have been impossible to have a person standing there all night dialling numbers, nor could they have tied up the fax lines during the day. The answer was, of course, to use the PCs as fax machines during the night. The database was loaded into the fax software, the time for send was programmed, and the pricelist that was to be sent that night was typed and loaded. This process took about 10 minutes to set up. During the night, the faxes were sent, and

supporting the business

the engaged or unobtainable numbers appeared as an exception report the following day.

Perhaps your business could use a PC-based fax, along with the many advantages in operating. By the way, the quality of fax sent was so much higher because it didn't need to be converted into digital format in the fax machine, it was already there in the PC. If your argument is that you send handwritten faxes sometimes, and so the fax machine must stay, consider a flatbed scanner for under £100 that can scan any document or photograph you need into the PC, and then fax it electronically.

email

This is perhaps the most talked about development in the market today, and the one piece of technology that will change the way you do business forever. We were part of the original email culture whilst working for IBM in the early 1980s. This large corporation developed its own form of email that was far beyond the competition at the time. Today, the Internet has grown to the extent that we can all access email for a very modest cost, and the development of the digital TV will mean that this can be used to send email as well.

So, what is this email? Well, electronic mail is simply the transmission of a piece of text to an address box that is owned by the intended recipient of the text.

To send email from your PC, you will need the following:

- a PC with a modem attached to it
- an Internet dial-up account, available from BT or an Internet provider who advertises locally in your area. Contact the Chamber of Commerce if you are unsure. These cost from £7 to £14 per month to own, which you pay monthly to the Internet provider. This simply allows you to connect to the Internet, and you then pay for the local telephone call on your phone bill as usual.
- an email account, which will allow you to have your own mailbox with your name, or an abbreviation of your name. This comes with the dial-up account.
- a piece of software usually free from the Internet provider.

Having approached an Internet provider, they will usually help you to get started, so don't be too put off by the jargon, it's really very easy indeed.

So, now you are connected, and the world is your oyster. If you now look carefully at the business cards that people give you, you will see their email address listed alongside the office number, the mobile number, etc.

Using the email system becomes a habit. It is a very quick way of communicating where the telephone has failed. It is also very private, as the individual's email is usually restricted to them alone, and so, unlike a fax, the contents are delivered to the reader in a direct way.

When you get proficient at the basics, you will learn that it is possible to attach documents to the email itself. This is where the fun starts. The

> **Using the email system becomes a habit.**

document can be anything from a Word or AmiPro document of whatever size, to an Excel spreadsheet or a PowerPoint presentation. By using the email as the train, you can add carriages of documents from one to many, and send the lot to the intended reader. The great news is that the reader can not only open the documents if he/she has the correct application, but that the document can be changed and saved.

We use email more than ever today, for sending draft documents around the world for approval or change. The amended files come back within a few hours in the same format, whereupon we can print them off or simply forward them to another email user. If your business has more than one office, or if you have remote sales staff, then this method of working can be very efficient.

We attended a presentation some months ago where, once we had arrived at the venue which was over 200 miles away, we found the diskette with the PowerPoint presentation was saved on the wrong version. Instead of panic setting in as the audience of 200 assembled, we simply had our office email another copy, this time saved in the correct

> **Email will change your business lives.**

lower level format. The email arrived, the file transferred and the show went on without a hitch.

Email will change your business lives if you integrate it into your business and use it in general work, but there is just one word of caution. The email is not a formal letter, it is not a telephone call, and it is not a fax that others can read. In fact, email can become a very informal medium, which can be damaging in itself. Be careful not to become overfamiliar in the tone that you and your staff adopt. Prohibit the flippant use of email, particularly as your business gets bigger, and *never* use the email for important things.

In our own business, on more than one occasion, our management team used email for the announcement of staff promotion or staff leaving either voluntarily of more often by company request. This type of information will have an effect upon teams of people and individuals, and must be delivered by the manager directly. Using email will exacerbate the issue, creating a feeling of 'they don't really care' or simply fuel unwelcome discussion or rumour.

The Internet

There are probably few people who have not heard of the Internet, but many who have never had the opportunity to access it. The Internet itself is not a product or a service, but simply a collection of many computers around the world, linked by telephone connections.

No single person or government owns the Net, nor is it governed in any way. The information held on these computers can be made available to anyone who wants to look, and therefore anything can be published including audio, video, images, pictures and text. Much discussion revolves around pornography on the Internet, which is about as available as it is in your corner shop or newsagent's. The issue is whether you can accidentally stumble across it, and the answer is 'very unlikely'. The bulk of material on the Internet is both informative and useful. We use the Internet today as a huge source of knowledge, the first point of research about anything and everything.

> We use the Internet today as a huge source of knowledge.

You can search for any subject on Earth with a key word, for example, or you can follow structured paths defined in the software that you use to browse.

In business, you may find that your suppliers publish information that they no longer print, like old technical guides or indeed new technical guides. In our last business, the on-line pricing and discount codes were invaluable in preparing our own quotes from the suppliers we used. If needed we could then turn that electronic enquiry into a real order and confirm it at the press of a button.

So, you can know see that value of the Internet. It is a massive and unlimited library of knowledge, as well as a forum for the conducting of real business, a business you will come to know as E-commerce or electronic commerce.

As a business owner, it is vital that you spend a little time getting to know how to use the Internet. If you don't have time in the working day to get along to the IT competence centre in your local Business Link, try using the cyber-café in your local town. If you explain that you are unfamiliar with the Internet, you will usually get friendly help from the staff who will demonstrate and show you how to use the system. It will take you minutes to learn and a lifetime to use, so get started soon!

Web pages

Before we leave the Internet as a subject, it is worth spending a few lines introducing web pages. This is the protocol by which you are able to publish on the Internet, and so a page of text straight from a word document, once converted to a code we call HTML, can be termed a web page. Once you spend any time on the Net, you will be looking at other people's web pages, and you will notice that they contain pictures, graphics that move, artistic words and layout, and forms for you to fill in.

With an increasing frequency, you will be invited to publish your own web page about your business, and for a few hundred pounds a web page company will offer you this service. *Never* simply reprint your corporate information and call it your web page.

By looking at the Internet, you can search for your competitors and market players, and notice their pages. Find the ones that excite you, the ones you like, and then note the style, colours, design, and complexity. Notice how many seconds it takes to download, and how easy it is to get the information that you want. A web page is not a brochure, and it is not a television production. It is something unique and different, and must be approached with no preconceptions.

Decide what you want your web page to do. We used our page simply to solicit enquiries, using a special form that you could email to us from the page itself. Others use them to raise awareness of the business, and some go the whole way and try to sell you something directly from the site. Be specific and don't rush; there are lots of bad web sites out there, but the ones that work are the ones that are well thought out.

The use of databases for marketing

For less than £100 you can purchase customer contact databases that you can use in your business. As a small business, it is likely that you have card index systems, or have used something like Outlook or similar. The recording of information about a customer can be extremely valuable in the ser-

supporting the business

251

vicing of this client. Some databases allow you to schedule a future telephone call with a contact, and a beep alarm goes off in your PC when the appointed time arrives. You need never forget a customer again!

Sales notes are invaluable, particularly when sales staff are absent or unavailable. The call recipient can simply access the database, and quickly learn the last action, intended activity, and the prices quoted.

Most packages allow automatic letter entry and faxing direct to the customer at the press of a button or two, and the accessing of complex information is never easier. If you ever mailshot your customer base, or indeed some of the customer base, the adding of search words to the contact can allow you to search for all customers who have bought widget A, for example if you wanted to sell an upgrade to them. Alternatively, the segmentation of the customer base, to mail information only to the customers in the Leeds, Derby and Chelmsford areas, which is where those product sales staff are based, may be useful.

Once the information is entered, it opens a whole range of possibilities for search and segmentation, recording and classification. We would firmly recommend that you invest in a sales contact database early in the development of your business, as it will certainly return to you manyfold in the future. A last word of advice is that whether you adopt a computerized database or not, the Data Protection Act will apply to you if you simply keep records. Enquire of either Business Link, or your solicitor, who will advise you properly.

Management information

As your business grows, it will become useful to be able to analyze information about all sorts of aspects of your business. The obvious ones are covered in Chapter 5: 'Sales and marketing strategies', but also in the financial analysis of your performance.

Sales by product, by postcode, by salesman, by month, are all aspects of the business that will be tested from time to time, and having this detailed knowledge will be a powerful management tool indeed.

It is sometimes recorded within your accounts package, particularly if you use the purchase order and sales order processing. Using ODBC software, it will be possible to pivot this information into Excel and play with it in any form that you desire.

If not, then you should give some thought as to how best to record this information for future use. General PC applications, such as Excel or Access, can be made to handle this sort of data very inexpensively. Remember to only enter the data once, otherwise you do not have the most efficient set-up.

The hidden costs of support in your business – training

As with any technology, there is a period of learning when you first implement within your business. It is a natural reaction to discount training as an unwelcome expense, and to get by with hands-on style learning. We can assure you that when this happens you will never get the true potential of the technology to work for you.

We have seen some serious misunderstandings of the use of technology in the past, which in some cases has completely negated the technology itself. It is not uncommon for a computer network to be purchased for the first time, and then for all the staff to accidentally save any documents they produce in their local PC drives. The fileserver, that is meant to hold all the files so that they can be shared and secured and backed up, sits there with nothing to do. A simple training course would have alleviated this problem, and have saved a large amount of management time in trying to resolve the issues.

> You must embrace training as a productivity issue.

It is a common statistic that for every 12 PC users in your office, one person, on average, spends half their time in work volunteering to help the other users. It is quite startling just how much time can be wasted because of poor training approach within some quite large businesses.

In small business, you cannot afford these ratios, and you must therefore embrace the training available as a productivity issue and not simply a cost line. If you contact your local TEC (Training Enterprise Council, subsidized courses, as well as grant assistance in some cases for the training of staff in IT, are available.

Video conferencing

It would be remiss of us if we were to close this chapter without discussing the advent of video conferencing. As the ISDN telephone lines get less expensive, and the cable operators gain a footing, the technology for video conferencing from your PC will arrive.

supporting the business

253

Indeed, this technology is available today, and has been used for some time by the middle-sized business and certainly by the corporates. In Manchester a private network has been funded in conjunction with the Chamber of Commerce, which will promote the use of video conferencing between small business. So, you see the future has already arrived!

Video conferencing will get less expensive.

You may not see the instant attraction of using video conferencing in your own business, but imagine if your customers had the facility, and consider the following:

- less travel, particularly to suppliers
- environmentally friendly way to do business
- less expensive than driving and parking, particularly when toll roads and toll city centres are introduced
- ideal if your business has multiple sites
- better than just a telephone
- overseas clients feel closer to you, even if they haven't met with you
- no airfares, train fares, hotel costs, etc.

Video conferencing will get less expensive and more widely adopted within the business community in the coming years, and it is a service that your business link can demonstrate for you.

Where to get impartial advice on how to buy technology

Well, so far in this chapter we have mentioned the Business Link rather a lot, which is because they have IT competence centres within most main Link offices. If your needs are specific, you can always contact the vendors of this equipment directly for demonstrations, etc.

If your need is for truly impartial advice, the use of an independent consultant will be your best option. In a technology purchase, the total costs are almost always increased at the end of the project, due to something that has been missed, or forgotten. A well-briefed consultant can make this process of technology selection and purchase a whole lot easier and more cost-effective. Ensure that you instruct your consultant in terms of what the end result will do, what it will solve and what direct and indirect benefits the business will gain.

Summary

We have attempted to highlight just some of the technology that you will need to consider when developing your small business. The products described above will certainly add value to most businesses, and bring bottom-line benefits to your company's performance.

As we approach the Millennium, the development of new technology is relentless. The ability of a small business to use technology in order to leverage a part on the world stage of commerce has never been greater. The business that embraces technological advancements, but only actually adopts the ones that are right for the business, is the winning one.

Not all technology is right for you as an individual or as a business, but the decision not to use must be a conscious one. To discount through lack of knowledge is unacceptable, and to reject through a Luddite existence will do nothing to increase your chances of business success.

PRACTICAL STEPS

Spend a little time in the development planning of your business to understand the environment in which you operate, and gather up all the technological solutions that will give you a competitive advantage in your marketplace.

supporting the business

time and stress management

Organization of time

Prioritizing your activities correctly

Plan out your business issues

Change of mindset

This is one of the most important chapters of the book, according to many of our entrepreneur colleagues. How do you cope with running your business, managing your employees, and keeping your family home a happy and content one?

It seems almost an impossible feat for any one human to cope with – so how can you manage to successfully juggle the endless pressures and find the right balance?

■ Solution

Planning for future profits and worrying over people problems can be immensely stressful regardless of time, and can cause many a sleepless night for any business professional.

We found that if you can change the way you think about the business and actually run your business in a logical and methodical manner, we are absolutely convinced it will help you solve these problems.

There are three major steps to conquer stress and time constraints:

- organization of time
- planning out your business issues
- change of mindset.

ORGANIZATION OF TIME

We found prioritizing your time and planning your strategy can have a positive effect on stress. If done correctly, you can manipulate your time to ensure that family life does not suffer, whilst ensuring the business also runs smoothly.

So, what are we talking about? We are talking about a time management priority system which includes planning for the future. This system takes the stress out of your trying to remember every little detail, and will enable you to plan ahead without making emotional decisions based on not having enough time to come to an effective conclusion.

> **We are talking about a time management priority system.**

We had a very informal way of writing and planning our daily and future activities, but it did ensure that we slept well and organized our lives effectively. To help you to adapt a system personal to your own requirements, we have written an organization of time schedule opposite. This gives you a model, which you might like to adapt, or use as it is.

However, if you prefer to make a more conscious effort to install a more active system to suit your very busy hourly lifestyle, we can suggest the use of a *Day Book*.

Take a hard-backed ruled book in which, at the start of the day, the date is put at the top of the page and underlined; then a list of all the activities to be included with a priority number indicating the order in which the items should be completed. Use this book to record your every moment in writing. Record the phone numbers, the people you spoke to, the products you discussed and, most important, the prices you quoted over the phone. You will find an indelible record that will be forever valuable in the following days, and also later when you would otherwise remember talking to the person concerned, and the rough date, but cannot remember the product and price codes!

Whatever was not completed at the end of the day, transfer over onto the next page with the new date. This is quite a simple method and if, for instance, you are not in the next day because of sickness, your colleague can open up your day book and understand what needs to take place that day.

Whatever you do, after prioritizing your tasks, do not then decide to treat yourself, and do the 'nice' ones first. You can be tempted when you know that the others could take a longer time to complete or involve conflict or difficult calls. It is very satisfying to tick off a completed task, but it will not help your business in the long run if you are not tackling the urgent and important issues first!

In any time management book or course you will learn how to train yourself in what is important compared to what is urgent. To guide you, we have done our own summary on how to prioritize as follows:

ORGANIZATION OF TIME SCHEDULE   Date: 4/8/98

No.	Activity	Classify	Time scale	completed
1	Call J. Bloggs regarding his PC requirement	1	4/8/98	Y
2	Call Simpsons on supplying equipment to J. Bloggs	2	7/8/98	Y
3	Write up board report	3	8/8/98	
4	Send memo to T. Hill regarding packaging requirements for customer	4	6/8/98	
5	Sales letters to database regarding equipment available on discounted pricing	1	4/8/98	Y
6	Meeting with Terraxe – customer. Prepare brochure and presentation	3	6/8/98	
7	Reply to emails	2	5/8/98	Y
8	Call internal staff to arrange help on customer visit	2	5/8/98	
9	Check to see if delivery of goods have arrived to customer today	1	4/8/98	

No.	Project	Classification	Timescale	Completion
1	Design sales flyers for new product launch	2	12/9/98	
2	Slide presentation for sales team meeting	3	4/8/98	
3	Recruit new salesman	3	4/9/98	1st interview 14/8

PRIORITIZING YOUR ACTIVITIES CORRECTLY

■ **Important and urgent**

This activity should always be completed first. Normally, it would be a sales call to a customer, for example, or something which affects the profitability of the company. It must be tackled first thing before all other classifications. We normally classify it by denoting a 1 at the end.

■ **Important but not urgent**

This activity should be completed after the above classification. It normally entails an activity which is important for the company but does not have to be done quickly, e.g. a report for the board meeting. This can be fitted in after the first classification of important and urgent. Classification denoted by 2.

■ **Urgent but not important**

These are the activities which take up most of your time. Activities which need to be done immediately, but which are not important to the profitability of the company. Please note, if customers are involved, it is always important, so please classify correctly. If it is a supplier response and/or if it effects a sale, this activity must be classified 1 or 2.

Urgent but not important activities can be something that is considered for internal purposes, e.g., responding to mail, visitors and telephone calls; classified as 3 but sometimes required before classification 1, because a visitor or telephone call cannot wait.

These activities have to be done in line with your job position. These classified 3's are made urgent, and therefore you can sometimes forget if they are really important and should be done after. See if you can resist completing these tasks first and inform people that it will take you a day or so to complete; see if they can wait. It's surprising how many people will say, OK!

■ **Not urgent and not important**

These activities always seem to go down to the bottom of the pile and are things such as filing and long-term projects, which do not have to be completed that week. Classified as 4.

The above should help you prioritize correctly when organizing your daily tasks.

supporting the business

> *Remember – even if you have so much work to do that you can't fit it in between 8am and 6pm, just make sure you have completed the urgent and important tasks first and work conscientiously down your list. Leave work and continue your list the following day.*

You must also note that it is highly unlikely that you will get through the whole of your list for the day and it is very normal to write a list longer for the following day as you add on the tasks which are brought forward.

Important and urgent	Important but not urgent
1	2
Urgent but not important	Not urgent and not important
3	4

PLAN OUT YOUR BUSINESS ISSUES

It is easy to say 'Handle your stress by controlling your time', but there are other worries on an entrepreneur's mind apart from time. It is how to handle a difficult employee or how to manage your cash flow in order to pay your employees' salaries that month! These are the stresses and worries which you cannot solve with a simple time management sheet.

The simplest approach we found and one which works very effectively is to *write down what you are thinking* and set out a logical but methodical approach to your problem. It sounds too simple to work, but we can assure you it does. It helps you to put everything into perspective and get on with living rather than worrying! Running your business should be enjoyable, and therefore controlling these worries should help to maintain your enthusiasm rather than finding yourself bogged down with work issues and losing energy and interest.

Running your business should be enjoyable.

Sometimes it is useful to off-load onto a partner, but we have found that completing the form opposite, or one of your own design, with your partner or close friend (for a second opinion) can really sort these issues out once and for all. Talking does help, but writing the problem down psychologically off-loads the responsibility from your shoulders and makes it an issue to be sorted out logically rather than emotionally in your mind.

REDUCE YOUR STRESS NOW – WRITE IT DOWN!

The problem (Write a clear and factual description).

My sales director is not committed to meeting his sales targets. He is not advising his sales team how to reach their individual targets and therefore morale is low.

What is the worst that can happen in this situation?

Sales director leaves, maybe taking salesmen with him. This will affect profitability of company for next 4–6 months whilst finding replacements.

Now accept this position.

(Understand it and then write actions in which you can allievate the above. Speak to legal or other third parties to understand your legal position if necessary.)

1   *Conduct review with sales director immediately and understand his level of commitment.*

2   *Sit in at sales team meetings and understand problems.*

3   *Get involved with sales and oversee director's work daily.*

4   *If above methods fail, and sales director is not committed, discipline.*

5   *Plan a recruitment drive for sales director/sales people.*

6   *Speak to solicitor regarding dismissal if required.*

7   *If sales director leaves, take over his position immediately.*

8   *Place FD in your position temporarily whilst sales director is replaced.*

9   *Keep momentum and morale in company up and support new recruits.*

10   *Oversee new sales director until position has passed its probationary period.*

Timescale for this problem to be resolved.

Immediately. If recruitment of a new sales director has to occur, then 3–4 months timescale.

---

supporting the business

You may find that Question 2, regarding the worst scenario, is a strange one. However, by writing this down, you have psychologically *acknowledged and accepted the worst outcome*, therefore relieving your fears and anxieties. You can see the problem logically and write down the actions in a formalized way, therefore avoiding any emotional decision-making, which you may regret at a later stage.

CHANGE OF MINDSET

We are delighted for you if you are already practising the above two methods. If you do not take on board the serious issues that will manifest as a result of stress, you could end up with difficulties both at work and at home. Stress is an overworked but often misunderstood issue, and must be taken very seriously by all practising entrepreneurs. Statistics show that difficulties in the home life of entrepreneurs is highly likely in this category of work occupation. So, take heed, all you entrepreneurs with families.

> Stress is an overworked but misunderstood issue.

Striking the right balance is often very hard but it is so important. We made sure the balance worked and ensured we were there for the children. Every evening we fed, bathed and put them into bed, had dinner and then, once rested, went to work on the business for a couple of hours at home instead of at work. It worked very well and as a couple we believed that 2 to 3 hours as a family every evening were just as important as working on the business.

Weekends were just kept for the family but evenings (if business called for it) were taken up with business matters. Normally 2 hours plus per evening, instead of watching television or reading a book. We agree that running a business meant that our hobby time *was the business*. During the weekends, we spent time with the children doing special things, like eating out or going for a 5-mile walk with a backpack of food to take in the scenery and relax our minds and bodies from the office environment.

Whatever ways you can find in making the balance work between business and family life, try to stick to a plan and make it happen every week. It is easier to work late every night and come home after the children are in bed, but this has to be negotiated with your partner first and to suit the whole family and not just your needs. Planning your family time is so important, and agreeing this sooner rather than later will help you be successful in your business in the long term.

■ **Solution**

> *We found that involving your life goals with your partner will help them to understand what you are trying to achieve. By placing both your personal, health and financial goals down, you can work together like you have never done before. It is so exciting as you see your hopes and dreams become reality as you forecast your future together.*

Setting timescales on your personal goals and the steps in how to achieve them ensures a successful partnership. It worked for us and I am sure it will help you too. Please find on page 266 our own personal plan (Fig. 12.4) categorized under three subject headings: personal, health, and financial.

Personal

This includes all the things you would like to achieve in the home: DIY, holidays, friends and personal development in the year.

Health

This is to include all the activities or hobbies for yourself and the family you would like to do in the year.

Financial

This includes house move, buying investments, or purchasing new furniture, increasing pension contribution, private education for children, new clothes, etc.

This form can also be adapted to your own personal preferences, so please feel free to modify it or change it completely to your own style. This form should be updated every month and your progress monitored and then a new goal sheet should be written again in the following year. We enjoyed writing our own personal goals on New Year's Eve, so that we could celebrate what we accomplished that year and toast the New Year with excitement and exhilaration and the wonderful drug called 'anticipation'.

supporting the business

GOALS FOR YEAR 1998

Personal goals	Timescale	Progress to date	Actioned by
1 Decorate all bedrooms	By end of summer		SW
2 Tile bathroom	By end of summer		PW
3 Clear out garage and have car boot sale	End of April		PW
4 Clean house from top to bottom	Every Saturday am		SW/PW
5 Choose one overseas holiday for family and book	Before May	Portugal and booked for July 18	SW
6 Organize two visits to family in children half term	End of April		SW
7 Visit two close friends and stay for weekend	January	May and August booked	SW
8 Go to evening classes to study law	Book to start in Sept		SW
9 Join business clubs relevant to occupation	Immediate	Find two clubs to date	PW
10 Take children to club events	Immediate	Brownies, Tennis	SW

Health goals	Timescale	Progress to date	Actioned by
1 Take children swimming	Every Saturday		PW
2 Take children for walk/bike ride	Every weekend		PW/SW
3 Go to yoga classes in the evening	Once a week		SW
4 Exercise on weights machine	Every evening for 20 min		PW

Financial goals	Timescale	Progress to date	Actioned by
1 Purchase new dining room furniture	September	Selected type	SW
2 Sell Woolwich shares to finance above	Summer		PW
3 Increase pension contributions by £50 each	Immediate		PW
4 Save PW's bonus and put into PEP	June		PW
5 Put Maria into nursery one afternoon a week	September	Selected nursery. Visit on 20/8	SW

Fig 12.4

15 WAYS TO RELAX

1   Make time for yourself. Schedule *me times* into every day. (For example, have hot bath in the evening, go for a massage, have your hair done, read a magazine/paper.)

2   Exercise regularly 20 minutes per day, 3 days per week. Exercise releases feel-good hormones into our bloodstream, lowers blood pressure, relaxes muscles and clears head. Try yoga if you are able to – it helps you to relax and strengthen back problems.

3   Learn to recognize what you can control and let go of what you can't.

4   Remember to mentally pat yourself on the back when you have accomplished something, no matter how small.

5   Avoid excessive alcohol, caffeine, fats and sugars and avoid smoking.

6   If you feel stressed because of the vast amount of responsibilities you have, maybe it's time to delegate.

7   Decide what your most productive time of the day is, and schedule most important tasks then. Don't waste that prime time on routine tasks that can be accomplished at any time.

8   Schedule important and urgent tasks first when energy levels are high.

9   In time we often consider wasted, sitting in the doctor's waiting room or driving, listen to a tape, read and try to switch off from work activities.

10 Don't waste your time and raise your stress level by reliving mistakes. Every mistake is a learning experience. Learn from it and move on.

11 Enjoy the people in your life who make you happy and allow yourself time with them.

12 If there are not enough hours in the day, maybe it's time to explore making lists and prioritizing goals. Talk with someone you know who successfully accomplishes a lot and ask for help. Visit the local bookstore or library for self-help material.

13 Laughter is often the best remedy for stress. Find reasons to laugh – a funny movie, a night out with friends, etc.

14 When you feel your temper rising, count to 10. This will give you time to calm down and keep you from saying something you might regret later. If 10 is not enough time to calm down, keep counting.

15 If you have had a hard day, take a hot bath or shower. You feel much better and relieve the tension after a difficult day. Then get out and do some exercise and get those feel-good hormones working.

PRACTICAL STEPS

- ■ **Organize your day by using a day book or form as illustrated.**

- ■ **Prioritize your time correctly, i.e. to what is really urgent and important.**

- ■ **Plan out your worries – reduce your stress now!**

- ■ **Share your life goals with your partner and write them down together.**

supporting the business

The 20 immutable

1. Build your company on a firm foundation, by implementing a shareholders' agreement with key business objectives.

2. Plan to succeed by producing a detailed business plan, which must be updated annually. Ensure your plan has accurate cash-flow projections and forecasts.

3. Resource your business carefully to gain advantage. Keep overheads to a minimum and make savings on all purchases to increase profits.

4. Stay customer focused in everything that you do. Understand their needs and develop good, long-term relationships. Remember, nothing happens until you make a sale!

5. Ensure flexibility in your commitments to long-term contracts such as building leases. Be imaginative at all times when structuring your business.

6. Separate your personal and business liabilities and try not to guarantee your business dealings with personal assets or contracts.

7. Maximize the grant assistance available to you at all times. Be aware of all local and regional schemes for loans and employment opportunities.

8. Train yourself continuously and increase your learning ability as often as you can. Develop your knowledge to assist you in the future running of your business. Join business clubs, go on seminars, training courses and read magazines, Sunday papers, *Financial Times* and business books.

9. Cash is the most important resource in your business. Ensure you are fully aware of how to control and increase your working capital. Check regularly and maintain accurate stock records. Keep

laws of business

10 Never take your eye off the sales ball. Liaise with sales department daily, and always get involved with the customer if there are any issues.

11 Make every employee a sales representative as part of his or her job function. First impressions last.

12 Control your business by effective board meetings and trained direc tors.

13 Understand what it is that you sell and to whom. Know what your Unique Selling Proposition is and tell the world.

14 Retain your customers at all costs and remember you are never too high in the company to communicate regularly with your customers.

15 Recruit the very best people that you can. Take on winners, and don't compromise.

16 Use SMART objectives to manage professionals so that employees understand the standards and can comply accordingly.

17 Appoint your professional advisors carefully and interview a selection before making your final choice. These advisors will be with you during your business term, so it is important to spend time and find the best one for your business.

18 Disposal of your business is a time of great risk and vulnerability, so be wary and check and recheck contracts. If you are not sure, go for a second or even third opinion.

19 Use information and IT effectively in your business to gain competitive ground.

20 Plan your life and business goals formally to conquer stress and time pressures.

useful books

Lintott, David (1990) *Handbook of Company Secretarial Administration*, ICSA.

Roberts, Wess (1993) *Victory Secrets of Attila the Hun*, Bantam Books.

Scrine, A.J. (1990) *Be Your Own Company Secretary*, Kogan Page.

useful addresses

British Venture Capital Association
Essex House
12–13 Essex Street
LONDON WC2R 3AA

CBI
Centrepoint
103 New Oxford Street
LONDON WC1A 1DU

Institute of Directors (IOD)
116 Pall Mall
LONDON SW1 5ED

British Chamber of Commerce
Manning House
22 Carlisle Place
LONDON SW1P 1JA

BDO Stoy Hayward Consulting Ltd
Peter House
St Peter's Square
MANCHESTER M1 5BH

The Entrepreneur's Club
P.O. Box 5217
Hatton
DERBY DE65 5ZF

Federation of Small Businesses
2 Catherine Place
Westminster
LONDON SW1E 6HF

Albert Humphrey
Team Action Management Consultant
1 Randolph Crescent
Little Venice
LONDON W9 1DP

index

The Entrepreneur's Club

The new club for all entrepreneurs and business owners

One of the hardest parts of running your own business as we have found, is that there is no one out there to lend an ear or give you some good sound advice.

To alleviate this problem faced by all entrepreneurs and business owners, we will be setting up a unique club which will be operated in two ways. Firstly, we would like to operate a dedicated website to allow members to interact freely on the Internet. This may be extended, depending on demand, to offer a telephone-based support service.

Secondly, we can offer you membership to a professional but relaxed and friendly small business club particular to your region. It would give you the chance to meet other business entrepreneurs at regular intervals, talk within friendly surroundings, arrange benchmarking visits and organized lectures, particpate in social get-togethers etc. Such positive interaction will help your small business grow and maintain a healthy and successful presence in your region. You will also find it helpful talking to people who have gone through the same problems, therefore reducing your personal stress levels and time restraints.

If you are interested in joining this quite unique small business club, please complete the tear-off reply coupon below and send to the following address:

The Secretary, The Entrepreneur's Club, PO Box 5217, Hatton, Derby DE65 5ZF.

We look forward to starting The Entrepreneur's Club as soon as possible and therefore urge you to reply immediately – please do not delay.

The Entrepreneur's Club: application for membership

Title (Mr/Mrs/Ms) _____ First name _____ Surname_____

Position_____

Company name and address_____

_____ Postcode_____ Email address _____

Nature and type of business _____

Are you starting up?   Yes/no

If no, what is your annual turnover? _____

Address to respond to (if the address is different from above) _____

_____

_____ Postcode_____ Email address _____